M ovement and Learning in the Early Years

Supporting Dyspraxia (DCD) and Other Difficulties

Christine Macintyre
and
Kim McVitty

P·C·P

Paul Chapman Publishing

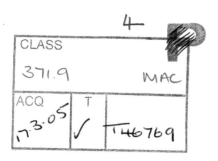
© Christine Macintyre and Kim McVitty

First published 2004

 Paul Chapman Publishing
A SAGE Publications Company
1 Oliver's Yard
55 City Road
London EC1Y 1SP

SAGE Publications Inc.
2455 Teller Road
Thousand Oaks, California 91320

SAGE Publications India Pvt Ltd
B-42, Panchsheel Enclave
Post Box 4109
New Delhi 110 017

Library of Congress Control Number: 2003116896

A catalogue record for this book is available from the British Library

ISBN 1 4129 0236 3
ISBN 1 4129 0237 1 (pbk)

Typeset by Pantek Arts Ltd, Maidstone, Kent
Printed in Great Britain by Cromwell Press, Trowbridge, Wiltshire

Contents

Acknowledgements

Our thanks go to all those who have shared their thoughts, concerns and experiences both happy and sad for these are the things that made this book possible. Thank you to all the children who tried out activities and evaluated our plans. Some will see themselves in the book and we hope they are pleased. Lastly a speical mention to David Barrington who gave us ideas and who helped prepare resources for the activities that were suggested as support strategies in the text. Thank you all.

Preface

This book is written to support parents and practioners who wish to understand movement and how it contributes to all aspects of learning – intellectual, social and emotional, as well as the movement/motor aspect itself. Moreover, as there is a huge increase in the number of children with movement learning difficulties (Keen, 2001), that is children who do not move confidently and easily, the book also highlights the significant part less competent movement plays within the specific learning difficulties, e.g. dyspraxia, dyslexia and the attention deficit disorders (ADD), and with hyperactivity (ADHD).

Why is movement so important?

From the very earliest age, being able to move confidently and efficiently in many environments underlies most, if not all, activities of daily living. An interesting claim by Laszlo and Bairstow (1985) in fact is that 'all *overt* behaviour is expressed through movement' and while this gives us pause for thought, it also begs the question, 'How are we to know if children have learned if they don't move?' Considering possible answers also demonstrates that 'movement' is much more than physical education, important though that is. It is part of writing and mathematics; it is essential in getting dressed, in using a knife and fork, even in being able to speak. It is part of communication both verbally and through touch and so it is fundamental to the achievement of a whole plethora of social skills. Moreover, movement allows children to do what they want to do, in other words to control their environment, and thus is essential to their becoming more independent. Being able to carry out activities such as tying laces, catching a ball or riding a bike just as well as and at the same time as their friends makes a huge contribution to a child's self-esteem. This in turn impacts on how confidently they approach and complete all kinds of learning tasks. All of these precursors to learning are discussed in the book.

It goes without saying that all the adults who interact with young children want them to do well in all aspects of their living and learning. For a very few children, providing a movement environment with resources that stimulate them to achieve and progress can be enough to ensure a good start. Many more require consistent and considered support and encouragement if they are to realise their potential and some need specialised resources and a high level of help. Providing the most appropriate level and kind is a complex endeavour and to be most effective it has to come in the early years, i.e. ideally pre-school, certainly before age 8. This is because appropriate support can reduce the effects of difficulties, sometimes even before the children realise that they are there. Moreover, if the difficulties persist, then the parents and teachers may well have established shared ways of helping in a positive, child-centred environment.

What is involved in providing this support? Parents and practioners must be able to observe young children as they move and assess whether their development is proceeding according to established 'norms'. (Examples of age-related norms are provided in Appendix 1.) If it is, they must know how to extend a child's learning through the provision of challenging activities; if it is not, if progress is accelerated or delayed, they must observe even more closely, then analyse the child's movement patterns, assess what is amiss and provide or seek effective and timely support.

This may present a huge challenge for parents who suspect difficulties when their children are in the age range 0–3, but they are the experts, the children's first educators and they are right to be persistent in asking for help.

CASE STUDY

Marie, Freya's mum explains:

'I knew from the start there was something wrong. Freya was so floppy; it was obvious that although she looked fine when lying in her cot, she had very little strength in the top of her body. Her arms just hung limply down and she could hardly suck. I had to dribble milk into her. However, the doctors didn't seem perturbed. "Just give her time," they said, but I knew she needed more than that. So I rubbed her little arms gently and made her close her fingers round a rattle and encouraged her to squeeze the sponge in the bath. These were all games that she enjoyed and we felt we were doing something to encourage her development. We stimulated her but it took a lot of thinking and wondering if we were doing the right thing. Parents shouldn't be left alone like this.'

This early time is critically important for this is the time when children are developing their basic movement patterns, the foundation stones for more complex skills. Literally they are 'finding their feet' in a sheltered environment when parents or carers are there to prevent bumps and bruises and keep the children safe. And as the children learn to move they are developing all other facets of their learning – they are making decisions about where to go and if it is safe, who will be there and how to attract their attention, as well as what they are going to do to achieve their aim. So moving around is a problem-solving experience, which is the basis of intellectual, social and emotional competence. At this early stage attitudes to encountering new activities are being formed. It is important that they are positive ones.

Concerns like this may have promoted the compilation of curriculum documents for nursery and school-age children in the different regions. Two examples are *Curriculum Guidance for the Foundation Stage* (DfEE, 2000) and *A Curriculum Framework for Children 3–5* (SCCC, 1999) and these provide advice on the kinds of competences that should be nurtured in the early years (see also Appendix 2). Although these differ slightly in where the different skills are placed (e.g. in England, mathematics has a section of its own while in Scotland mathematical learning in the early years is subsumed under 'Knowledge and understanding of the world'), the key learning outcomes are essentially the same. These frameworks have provided critically important guidance in the selection of recommended activities and strategies within the book. In turn these should augment practioners' plans for their individual children in their own learning context.

The 'rewards' from helping children become 'better movers' are enormous. Just as poor movement is public and open to scorn, so improved movement is immediately visible and gains well deserved praise. It can be a source of happy communication with parents and carers, but perhaps listening to the children brings the best reward of all.

Scott, who has enjoyed his time in his perceptual-motor programme, explains, 'I'm much happier at school now because I can run faster and my friends let me play football now'.

*I*ntroduction

This book aims to help all those who interact with young children to:

- understand the importance of movement as a key factor in personal, social, emotional and intellectual development;

- observe movement patterns and assess/analyse them to identify any cause for concern;

- devise appropriate and enjoyable strategies and activities that will support the development of efficient and effective movement;

- justify including more movement activities at home and in the early years' curriculum.

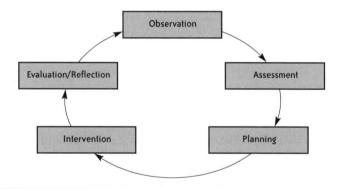

Figure 1 The cycle of observation and support.

Why are all of these skills so important?

At home, at school and during all of the activities in between, movement underlies most, if not every, aspect of learning. All the age-related feats of daily living, e.g. sucking to feed, reaching to grasp a toy, getting dressed, opening a lunch box, even speaking clearly, are compromised by not being able to make the correct movements plan, e.g. how to move, when to move and where to go. At school too, much of the curriculum is based on practical activities. The youngest ones must learn to spread toast or biscuits at snack, thread beads, complete jigsaws and gradually learn to become more independent. They must learn how to communicate with others and recognise how their non-verbal behaviour, another form of movement, is perceived and interpreted by others. All of these skills are necessary to cope with the vast number of activities involved in daily living. Every early movement experience promotes the development of the movement abilities such as balance and co-ordination, body and spatial awareness, which underlie the timely acquisition of more demanding tasks, e.g. more formal writing which requires a sophisticated amount of poise and control and mathematical problem-solving which involves recognition of shapes and symbols as well as numbers.

The slightly older children learn to manipulate materials in mathematics, science, environmental studies and music as well as coping with more demanding feats of co-ordination and body movement in physical education and drama. These are the more obvious 'movement things'. But movement is also a critically important, if subtle, part of learning to read, because the eyes have to work together in a controlled way to track the symbols on the page and when writing means copying from the board another more complex form of tracking is required. Writing itself is a major motor skill dependent on balance co-ordination, rhythm and control. And so, although many parents seem more concerned to find out whether their children can read and write and count to ten than asking about their movement skills, this could be a costly mistake. Perhaps they are overlooking the fact that movement competence is at the root of many different kinds of intellectual, emotional and social success.

If children are to see themselves as 'coping well' and gain confidence from their self-evaluations, they have to be able to move with confidence in different environments and with different 'tools'. When they can't cope at the toilet or do up their buttons at the same time as their friends, their self-esteem takes a hard knock, for these 'movement things' are public and exactly what the children themselves like to be able to do. Moreover, parents and teachers and even friends have expectations that these competences will be achieved 'at the right time' and comparisons among youngsters can be part of the daily scene. This adds often quite unnecessary stress to the process of growing up, yet if delay is suspected then opportunities for timely and appropriate intervention should not be missed. This is arguably more important for movement than other skills for the reasons listed above and because:

developmental movement and gross motor deficiencies are a special case
for intervention strategies. This is because movement difficulties may be
more difficult to eliminate than other deficiency classifications. (Cowden
and Euston, 1991)

This is a very significant finding. If movement difficulties are indeed 'harder to eliminate' than others kinds of problems then the case for early and sustained intervention in movement cannot be denied. One of the key aims in early years' education is to 'increase children's understanding of how their bodies work and to have children practise the fine and gross movement skills which will keep them safe' (DfEE, 2000). This understanding and these competences have to be nurtured to allow them to 'use tools and equipment' (SCCC, 1999). If these aims are to be met, the underlying movement competences, e.g. balance, co-ordination and the movement planning which precedes their use have to be carefully and regularly assessed.

The earliest 'assessments' all children have are made by observing their acquisition of movement patterns, e.g. when they hold eye contact, when they smile, when they sit unsupported, if and when they crawl, when they walk, when they use the pincer grip and when they can grasp and let go. All of these skills are known as 'motor milestones' and when they are achieved at the right time, then adults can be reassured that progress is being made according to the norms of development (see Appendix 1). These early assessments should be made by adults observing children interacting in their own environment and carrying out their usual activities. This is a naturalistic form of assessment that should not distort the findings or cause any stress. Making records of the children's progress in this way is critically important for such notes can pinpoint difficulties that may be present or looming and alert adults that early support might be required. If these difficulties or delays are minor, then carefully selected practices may help them to be overcome quite quickly. If they are more profound or long-lasting, however, then a programme of activities can be devised and the most appropriate support can be given without delay. This text suggests ways of doing just that, i.e. through observing the children, analysing their movement successes and difficulties and suggesting the most appropriate ways to help. Naturally, the ethos of doing that would be in a child-centred environment, i.e. based on recognition of each child's developmental stage, their readiness to learn more and the provision of activities and resources to let that happen (for examples, see also Macintyre and McVitty, 2003).

Maturation and myelination

One of the trickiest assessments adults have to make is whether children have a 'real difficulty' or whether maturation will do the job by itself. There is no doubt that most children become more nimble and dexterous as they mature. This is because the limbs generally become longer and stronger and capable of more movement things. In addition, myelination of the axons – or insulation of the passageways in the brain, which ensures that instructions pass directly to the correct muscle groups that promote the action – may not be complete at an early age. This leaves the child with the appearance of being slow to respond or of having poor co-ordination. Once the coating is complete, however, all may be well. This is one reason why it would be inappropriate to issue labels indicating specific learning difficulties before the children are 6 years of age, i.e. the time when the myelination should enable them to move well. New research (Winkley, 2003) is claiming that myelination may not be complete till early adulthood, so there is always time for the children to progress (see Chapter 1). However, it is best to play safe and not be tempted to delay. Early experiences which 'have a profound influence on how our brains are structured and our minds develop' (Winkley, 2003) are best to be of the kind that nurture and enhance. Recognising that a programme of practices will not harm any child, but will be likely to benefit them all, is important too and should surely override any doubts as to whether intervention is advisable.

Movement learning difficulties

Many children, including highly intelligent ones, have movement learning difficulties, even if they do not have the 'label' developmental co-ordination disorder (DCD, dyspraxia or DAMP, i.e. a Scandinavian term coined to cover a disorder of attention, movement and perception). New research also highlights the movement aspect of dyslexia, Asperger's syndrome and ADHD (Henderson et al., 2001). Clear speech (articulation) also depends on movement, i.e. control of the fine muscles in the mouth, and so any lack of muscle tone there means that both the acquisition of speech and communication are affected (Macintyre and Deponio, 2003). Poor muscle tone in the sphincter muscles can mean that control of the bladder and/or bowel can be affected so that toileting skills are delayed. This shows how widespread are the effects of poor movement control and co-ordination.

Left-handed children may give the impression of being poorly co-ordinated and clumsy, not because they have a movement learning difficulty but because they are struggling to cope in a world where resources are mainly designed for right-handed people. Yes, they need resources such as left-handed scissors but they also need their parents and teachers to understand the different ways they tackle tasks such as cutting out and they need demonstrations when forming letters or knitting! Adults have to consider the kind of support left-handed children require. When children find activities difficult, they often feel inadequate. They rarely blame the tools or the demonstrations, yet these are often the source of the problem.

And of course there are the children who can climb and run and jump but who find it really difficult to be still. They have a movement control problem that needs to be supported too, else their learning will be disadvantaged by distractibility and they may land up alienating others as well as not understanding themselves. Craig (2002) claims that, for many children, 'being still is the hardest movement of all!'

So, if a difficulty is suspected, what is to be done? Finding the root cause of the children's problems is the first step. Perhaps the children have perceptual difficulties so that the information they take in through their senses misleads them in some way? Perhaps the children can't plan what it is they wish to do? If these were the difficulties, then the support programme would be quite different from that needed by the children with poor muscle tone. Yet both would be unable to carry out their movement patterns competently and first observations might mislead observers into thinking that the intervention programme should be the same. This is why detailed knowledge and understanding must underlie observation, the first step in providing support.

The number of children presenting with these temporary/permanent difficulties is increasing rapidly (Keen, 2001), or perhaps it is that more informed parents are seeking help. This being so, it is essential to have a much larger group of adults who have the necessary skills and resources to make accurate diagnoses and who are able to design strategies to support them all.

Parents very often ask, 'When the children's movement improves, will they be more able to cope with their maths?' While research evidence denies a *direct* link (Dobie, 1996), teachers who have had children involved in early movement intervention/perceptual-motor groups invariably talk of the 'vast improvement' that they see in each child's self-confidence. This helps them confront other learning challenges with the self-belief that says 'I can do it... I can do it well.'

And of course there are many children who would be described as 'good movers' who have difficulties with other aspects of the curriculum, notably writing and mathematical calculations. Instead of giving them more of the same in the form of repeated tasks or homework exercises, which often means more failure, movement programmes can give extra fun practice in planning, in problem-solving, in making spatial decisions. These are essential strategies in writing, in mathematics and in developing social skills. The important thing is that children participating in these programmes are concentrating on the underlying competences in order to reduce their difficulties. When they recognise the progress they have made, they are enabled to tackle learning in a positive, confident frame of mind.

For all of these reasons, this text aims to equip interested and concerned adults to have the understanding and confidence to give all the children in their care programmes of movement activities so that their movement prowess is developed to the full. It also tries to provide a rationale to equip people to provide clear answers to why early intervention is so important. I hope it does.

CHAPTER 1

Early intervention in movement and learning

Making the case

When Trevarthen (1977) and other researchers into child development made the hugely important claim that 50 per cent of all learning happens in the first five years, the case for early intervention could not be denied. A huge expansion in the demand for early childcare was matched by arrangements to ensure that the best possible learning environment was provided; the 5–14 curriculum in Scotland was extended to encompass 3-year-olds and funding was directed into the early years sector. Programmes that sought to compensate for any kind of disadvantage, e.g. illness, restricted experiences, special needs or unstable or disadvantaged backgrounds, were initiated in many regions. This was so that all children could begin their primary school education on the same playing field, as it were.

While this intensive teaching resulted in many children making remarkable and sustained progress, for some the effect didn't seem to endure and after an initial advantage, some still trailed behind the others who had not had the benefit of the intervention programme. This finding raised a number of issues. Many questions were asked, for example: 'Were these very young children not ready for the very different kind of learning to which they had been exposed? Was the content of what they were to learn – in some cases learning to write numbers and recognise letters – too bound by the teachers' sense of the curriculum that was to come? Would it have been better taking the children into a carefully structured environment and encouraging them to learn through play? Or was it the cultural shift that was too great? Were the home/school differences such that new school learning was dissipated or seen as inappropriate by the people and the experiences the children had at home? If so, how could these obstacles be overcome?

These kinds of questions are still critically important when claims in 2003 assert that the earlier children have 'experiences' the greater the impact on learning they will make. If proven, this 'has implications for drawing the 0–3-year-olds into the larger picture of the educational process' (Winkley, 2003). Doubts about whether such young children can be ready to absorb learning have been offset by the resurgence of the importance of critical learning periods and suggestions that if learning doesn't happen at the 'right time' it could be more difficult to assimilate, even be 'too late' and potential could be lost. These 'right times' are now thought to be when the brain is most open, i.e. before myelination is complete. This is in the period between 0–6 years.

Certainly this claim has been verified with regard to the visual system. Before age 5 every attempt is made to stimulate the children's vision in the knowledge that later, i.e. once the critical time has passed, it will be too late to stimulate a greater degree of vision. More recent findings point out similarities in the timing of emotional development. Over the years much insight has been gained on bonding and attachment in early relationships and the effect these have on the development of confidence and security in the child (Ainsworth, 1972; Bowlby, 1979). Now it is considered that early, positive parent/child relationships stimulate brain development, so there is an intellectual as well as a social/emotional gain. How can this be? Because as the relationship is formed, the parent acts as a container for the baby's very intense feelings, in times of stress soothing and calming the child so that a pattern of quieter 'acceptable' behaviour is established. The child then is enabled to internalise this template and make future adjustments without help. Moreover, these routines and repetitions help develop 'expectancies' which give structure and comfort to the child's day. With this in place, the children are freed to encompass new learning.

Early movement patterns too, are subject to this 'best time to learn'. Many, if not most, children with specific learning difficulties have not crawled and later attempts to teach them have largely been unproductive. It would seem that the time to acquire certain movement abilities, e.g. the cross lateral pattern which enables crawling to be achieved, appears to be time specific too. At first glance this would not seem to be a major hurdle because, after all, older children and adults don't crawl – except up stairs and up mountains! But learning to crawl is actually very important, because in so doing children learn about the space around them and discover how far and in what direction objects in their environment are. They learn to balance in a safe position and feel the transfer of weight from four balance points to three. They choose which hand is best to stretch and the first glimmerings of hand dominance are established. It can be seen then that crawling is much more than a movement pattern which has limited use. Children who have not achieved their developmental milestones at the correct time, however, cannot be faced with the idea that it is too late. They have to have extra support in the form of pro-grammes where the teacher replicates the specific stages of early development to 'try to set the neural clock to the correct time' (Goddard, 1996). These can be in any aspect of learning, e.g. movement, reading or whatever competence needs help.

The earlier these programmes can be put into place, the better. This is because in these earliest times the brain cells (neurones) adapt to circum-stances much more readily than later and so positive inputs from the environment, e.g. teaching, support, practice and praise, can help the part of the brain which functions well to take over from the 'disabled' part. This is why early intervention programmes with children who have sensory or physi-cal impairments have been so successful. There are vast implications here for children who are not referred to specialists until it is too late for any remedial programme to have the fullest impact. In 2003, the scarcity of children's refer-rals to specialists for diagnosis of possible specific learning difficulties is making this happen – a very worrying state of affairs. In some areas resources will not be provided until a report from a psychologist is provided. While par-ents are understandably angry, teachers and the psychologists themselves are also frustrated by the delay. Many parents are seeking private help because they recognise the negative effect of waiting. But what about the children whose parents cannot afford this or who consider that the kind of support on offer locally is not appropriate for their child?

What is happening in the neurological development of the brain to make this very early time so important?

For many years there has been argument about the proportional impor-tance of nature and nurture in designating what children could do. Generally the debate concluded by asserting that a blend of genetic and environmental factors was responsible for children's progress, but there remained a suspicion that despite the blend, the genetic factors or 'what the children brought to learning' was of paramount importance. In 2003, however, research denies that children's brains are pre-programmed in any major way and claims that they develop substantially through experience. Furthermore, the research shows that the very earliest experiences have the most profound effect on structuring the brain (Winston, 2003).

These findings have huge implications for education in terms of the provision that should be made, the resources that are required and the quality of the teaching necessary to understand what is possible and desirable with very young children. But how are parents and teachers to know if their chil-dren are learning and if their rate of progress is what should be expected? A first clue is to observe the children's movement, for this is their first way of demonstrating what they have learned. When they stretch out and grip without fumbling, it can be seen that awareness of their hands and an appreciation of distance and direction has been mastered. When they sit up unsupported, development of the muscles in the back is evident along with a sense of balance, and when they crawl using a cross lateral pattern they are demonstrating both developing co-ordination and rhythm. But even within these activities which are dependent on maturation, i.e. the sequential pattern of changes which are innate and don't depend on teaching, it is not difficult to appreciate how opportunity and experience are necessary to produce skill. Certainly teachers are finding that the movement prowess of children has diminished by not getting out of doors to play. To compensate, many are providing daily movement programmes or even just taking steps to ensure that opportunities to move are built into the daily curriculum. In addition, many authorities are being badgered to put physical education specialists back into all primary (stage 1) schools.

What then is happening as movement skills are learned?

Development of the brain

Learning as a stimulant that structures the brain

Figure 1.1 shows two neurones out of the one hundred billion nerve cells which work together to receive, analyse and act on information from both external, i.e. environmental sources, and internal feelings, i.e. pain, hunger and the different emotions. As different experiences occur, these neurones join into networks that work together as systems to facilitate specific functions such as vision or hearing, movement or paying attention. Now, although these systems are in different parts of the brain, they work together in a dynamic way so that the most effective and efficient learning/movement can occur.

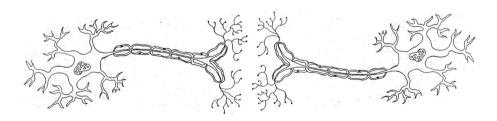

Figure 1.1 Two neurones with axons, dendrites and synapses.

Each neurone has an axon, a long spindle that leads to branching dendrites. These connect to other dendrites over a synapse, i.e. a gap, to approximately one hundred thousand other neurones. Chemicals such as dopamine act as neurotransmitters, passing messages from one cell to the next. The vast number of cells and connections mean that an infinite number of connections can be made and unmade. How does this come about?

The entire surface of the body is connected to the brain with different parts having their own number of neurones. Sensitive areas such as the hands, fingers and genitals have more neuronal connections. They are allocated much more 'brain space' than feet and legs. This means that activities such as playing the piano are good for reinforcing pathways as well as promoting finger awareness and so they promote other fine motor skills. As actions are repeated, the cell groups that have been used team up to reinforce specific pathways. This is done by a chemical change that ensures that a trigger to one cell will fire strongly to the next. This is called Hebbian learning and explains why habitual movements, i.e. those done regularly, can, after some initial practice, be performed almost automatically with little preparation or conscious thought. (Children with dyspraxia and other specific learning difficulties are likely to lack this automaticity.) As these pathways are established, the unused dendrites are discarded. This process is known as 'pruning of the dendritic arbor' (Bee, 1999). The commonly used 'use it or lose it' maxim may indeed be true! What is certain is that new experiences stimulate development of the brain.

Myelination – a sign of maturation of the brain

Myelin is a thin fatty coating that acts as an insulator around the axons, allowing signals to proceed smoothly and quickly to their designated ports. There is a gradual maturing of the brain that continues over thirty years but the 'majority of the maturation has occurred by the age of three to four years' (Winkley, 2003). This is how it is possible to begin to make fairly accurate prognoses about children's progress at this stage.

In the first months after birth there is a huge proliferation of synapse activity – the structures are anticipating experience and learning and getting the brain ready to absorb and retain it. The brain has prepared the paper for the script to be written upon it. All kinds of experiences contribute to this text. Interestingly, as areas become myelinated they mature and become more difficult to adjust. Old sayings such as 'You can't teach an old dog new tricks' may not be wholly true, but the adjustment may take longer!

Illnesses as well as the natural ageing process affect movement too. In patients with multiple sclerosis, as one example, this myelin sheath is breaking down. When this occurs, messages fire across to other neurones rather than along the correct path. This explains why control over the muscles is gradually lost and movement becomes jerky or flustered and confused before, in severe cases, the capacity to move disappears and the patient becomes wheelchair bound. In Parkinson's disease there is a paucity of dopamine and so the synaptic connections do not function well. This is one cause of the 'stopping' without reason, i.e. the cessation of movement, which is one symptom of the disease. It may also help to explain the tremor that defeats efficient movement.

And so the passage of the messages from the body to different parts of the brain are facilitated by the chemical transmitters and by the myelin coating which begins to be formed at three months and may, in a small number of cases, not be complete till early adulthood. Recognising this is important in the timing of making diagnoses of special educational needs or specific learning difficulties. It also has to be considered in giving a label to any child.

Sensory impact

The senses work together to provide sensory information (see also Chapter 3), which causes chemical change in the brain and alters the pattern of neuronal development. Gradually patterns known as working models or internal representations are formed. These are templates against which new opportunities can be evaluated. They provide a memory source allowing feedback and therefore informed choices in decision-making. Unfortunately some children seem unable to use feedback from one try to help the next. This may be linked to their having poor short-term memories.

The different parts of the brain

The different but interdependent parts of the brain (see Figure 1.2) develop at different times in a biologically programmed sequence. Newborns are dominated by the brain stem, as connections to the cortex are fragile at this stage. Part of the central nervous system, it is situated at the head of the spinal column and contains the nerve tracts which cross over to the opposite side. It is a primitive site shared by man, reptiles and fish. Damage to the core of the brain stem results in death (Goddard, 1996). Linked to the brain stem is the reticular activating system which monitors the sensory input and acts to calm or activate depending on what kind of response is appropriate. Children with ADHD and others who find it impossible to calm down may not be receiving the appropriate information to allow them to respond acceptably.

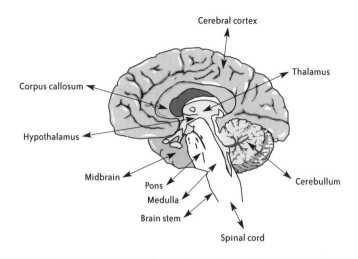

Parts of the brain	Functions
The brain stem (houses the pons and the medulla)	Regulates heart beat, breathing, blood pressure, the sleep/wake cycle, swallowing/feeding
The reticular activating system (within the central core of the brain stem)	Monitors the sensory systems
The pons and the midbrain	Organises the sensory, motor and autonomic systems
The thalamus	Organic sensory input
The hypothalamus	Controls hormonal function
The cerebellum	Interprets and acts on information to control output
The cerebral cortex	Two hemispheres with specialised functions; some tasks require the two halves to work together
The corpus collosum	Facilitates instant communication from one hemisphere to the other and allows the two parts to complement each other to produce complex outcomes; a screening device which can transmit or inhibit information

Figure 1.2 An outline of the brain with structures shown.

The pons and the midbrain link the brain stem to the cortex. These structures along with the thalamus and hypothalamus form the organising centres for sensory and motor input. The hypothalamus stimulates the output of hormones which control hunger and sexual/social behaviour. These are channelled into the pituitary gland that is often called the leader of the endocrine orchestra. The cerebral cortex works to inhibit this production. 'Out-of-control children' may lack this inhibition.

The cerebellum or 'little brain' is so called because, although it does not initiate thinking or movement by itself, it monitors signals from the motor centre in the brain and the nerve endings in the muscles. It controls the postural reflexes. It takes in a great deal of information and sends out the most appropriate cues. This is a very important area for movement. Any dysfunction in the cerebellum results in clumsiness and poor co-ordination.

The cerebral cortex is formed by two hemispheres linked by the corpus collosum. This allows messages to pass from one side to the other and so ensures integration and collaboration. While each side has specific functions, they are each dependent on the other for the successful completion of tasks. In males, the corpus collosum can be 40 per cent smaller than in females and so any damage may be harder to rectify. This finding gives rise to the notion that this could contribute to the larger number of boys who present with specific learning difficulties.

The left hemisphere is more efficient in processing information in a linear, sequential way, for language skills such as reading, writing, spelling, verbal memory and analytic reasoning, receptive and expressive speech. It identifies details and copes with changing information. Fine motor control is housed here also.

The right hemisphere is the base for social and emotional interactions. It is powerful in recognising faces and the emotional overtones of others. It is superior in visual perception and making spatial decisions. It is often said to be the artistic side of the brain. It regulates powerful and enduring feelings such as those that impact on self-esteem. This in turn has a critically important role in the development of attitudes towards living and learning.

And so early experiences are vital in all aspects of living. It is important that teachers and parents work together to maximise the opportunities their children have in the very early years. If one environment could be an extension of the other with the same provisos, i.e. providing an optimal level of support (neither isolating nor overcrowding) so that the children could be enabled to maximise their learning in a comfortable context, then surely their self-esteem would be kept high? Perhaps having a high self-esteem is the most important advantage of all?

Self-esteem

All parents and all professionals should strive to enhance the self-esteem of children in their care, yet it is not an easy thing to do, especially if the children are sensitive, vulnerable or consider themselves 'different' in any negative way.

What do parents and teachers need to know to enable them to support the children in a positive, yet realistic and unemotional manner?

The first thing is to understand what self-esteem is and how the contributing factors fluctuate as the children grow. Parents of children with difficulties are often encouraged to hear that 'making and keeping a friend' – one of the mainstays of self-esteem – very often becomes easier as the children mature. This is because as they grow and become more capable of understanding relationships, the children's perception of what is important in a friend changes. The children become less tied to external characteristics as they make judgements about each other and begin to value the internal traits of dependence, openness and honesty, i.e. competences not directly affected by 'being different.'

But there are all the primary school years to be lived through before that happens. Despite all the work done on anti-bullying in schools and homes, it still goes on. This highlights the importance of establishing self-confidence in the children as soon as it is possible to do so. But as children are all different in their aptitudes as well as in their contexts for learning, how is this to be done?

Analysing the self-concept

First of all there is the self-concept which is the overriding picture the children hold of themselves (see Figure 1.3). This is built up over time by the responses children perceive from those around them – the significant others or the most important people making the biggest impact. In the pre-school years parents and family members usually hold this role but when schooldays arrive, then the teacher often becomes the most important person in the child's life. Later this changes and the peer group take precedence. This is the 'must have the same things at the same time' era which imposes its own kind of strain. Most children want to be just like the others in their class and are devastated when, in their own eyes, they fall short of some unwritten norm. Other children 'are quick to spot any differences and the vulnerable ones get picked on, till any self-belief they have is in tatters' (parents of a girl with dyspraxia). Later, post adolescence, the parents often come into their own again.

The growing experience of other situations is critically important also. A child growing up in a supportive environment and enjoying the adulation of parents and friends may feel quite confident until other experiences, e.g. the reactions of those beyond the family group, act against the child's self-beliefs. Then the evaluative part of the self-concept, the self-esteem, comes into play. Children observe and make judgements based on how they think others value

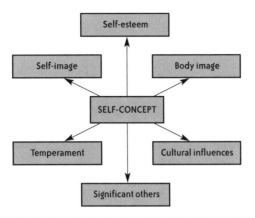

Figure 1.3 Self-concept.

them. Children with movement learning difficulties most often have a poor self-esteem and this has usually been attributed to repeated failure to do things successfully. Payne (1998), however, finds that 'failure in itself does not mean a low self-esteem. It is the way the significant others view that failure that is important.' Perhaps more thought needs to be given to how others react in both verbal and non-verbal ways for any 'failure' must be kept in proportion. There are many school skills that will never be needed again. It is a great pity if learning is spoiled by over-emphasis when children find activities difficult to do.

An important part of the self-concept is the body image, i.e. the children's pleasure in, acceptance of or disgust with their own physical bodies. At an increasingly young age, many children decide they are poor shadows of their role models and fall into debilitating illnesses such as anorexia in an attempt to alter their appearance. While the media concentrates on having 'exquisite' role models, the 'all that glitters is not gold' maxim is not likely to override the visual impact on the psychology of sensitive young people.

The self-esteem then is really a tri-dimensional image, i.e. 'what I think of myself depends on what I think you think of me'. Cooley (1962) called this the 'looking-glass self'. At the root of the evaluation is the children's perception that might or might not be accurate in the eyes of onlookers, but be critically meaningful to the children themselves. The self-esteem then is the distance between the children's evaluation of themselves and what they see as their ideal self.

Having a positive self-concept will, to some extent depend on the temperament of the individual children, the resilient ones being less likely to sustain hurt by the number of times negative vibes are encountered. If these are repeated, however, especially by those who are significant others at that time, reinforcement occurs. Then self-belief flounders and self-esteem falls.

In the early years, as parents are the most significant others in the children's environment, they have the first opportunity to help their children build a positive self-esteem. If the ways they do this can be shared with the teachers who will probably take over this role, then the children can avoid the confusion arising from the cultural shift caused by different sets of 'rules' and ways of interacting operating at home and at school.

Sound teacher/parent relationships can lead to parents being willing to share information about any vulnerability they see in their child. This prior knowledge allows teachers to take early steps to boost the children's confidence and thus avert bullying. After all the teachers will have thirty or so other children to care for. Any help they can have is invaluable. Sometimes when the relationship between the parents and the teacher is sound, other strategies to reduce any sense of being different can be tried, even unconventional ones.

CASE STUDY 1.1

Elena, Grace's mum, explains how her daughter has been helped:

'Grace, who is ten, has dyspraxia and dyslexia. She has recently moved to a very caring school where she has an individual spelling programme. Each night she has to learn three words although the others in the class have twenty or so. The teacher always has one of these words in the class list and that is the one she asks Grace to spell out loud in class. She marks it with an asterisk in her homework book so that we know that that is the important one if she can't manage the three. It's the same with maths. Her special sums are written at the top of the page and she has to concentrate on these. Sometimes the teacher even marks her sums right when they're not! This is just so that she can tell the other in the playground that she got ten out of ten. Grace doesn't look back at them anyhow and she is so pleased to see ticks on her page. She has to get her own special sums right though.'

'With this teacher Grace doesn't mind going to class although the playground is still difficult. Even although she would be allowed to stay inside that makes her different, so she pretends to want to go out, but when she does, nobody will play with her. She has a special notebook and sometimes she writes "Help, Help,

Help" and we are devastated that we just don't know how. We just have to try to take one day at a time and not worry her about the future. I tell her that nobody in the street is going to ask her the answers to times tables and she smiles at that. Her self-esteem is so low, she believes she's no use at all even although she is a lovely caring girl and we constantly tell her how much we love her.'

Being bullied

Every parent's worst nightmare (after abduction and abuse) is that their child will be bullied. Despite many attempts to rid schools of this menace, it seems to persist and vulnerable children are usually the ones that are picked on. Very often these are the children who find it difficult or impossible to run and jump or kick a ball, highly valued skills in the early years. Moreover, these are the children who are fearful of the consequences which they anticipate 'could happen'. There is no easy solution as each bullying scenario happens in a different context with different age groups of children (see Table 1.1) and many live in a miasma of fear.

Schools are proclaiming that bullying will not be tolerated but of course it is difficult to catch bullies who are adept at hiding their devious name-calling sessions, even their acts of intimidation or violence. Yet strategies to outwit the bullies are being tried in every school in a wholehearted attempt to rid the school of this problem.

Olweus (1995) defines a bully as 'one who repeatedly torments some other child with words, gestures, intentional exclusion from a group or physical aggression'. In Sweden where this research took place, he claimed that 9 per cent of children were regularly bullied. He found that victims had certain characteristics such as sensitivity and low self-esteem and had great difficulty in asserting themselves. They tend to accept rather than negotiate which 'turns other children off'. Olweus claims that bullies have little empathy with the victim's pain and this makes explanations and sharing feelings less than

Table 1.1 Changing patterns of bullying

Age 2–4	Takes toys; pushes or bites; little empathy developed
Age 4–5	More sustained physical attack; beginning of groups who bully
Age 5–6	Name-calling; threats to cause hurt but less physical hurt
Age 6–8	Sly bullying; taunts and destroying property happen when no one sees

useful. Moreover, he found that bullies are not basically insecure children who have developed a hard exterior to cover their anxiety – a commonly held view. He discovered that very often bullies have low levels of insecurity and anxiety. They enjoy terrorising their peers. They relish the power and the buzz. These theories make it even harder to form effective strategies to help.

Strategies to overcome bullying

From the first day in nursery children are encouraged to be kind to one another and are helped to understand sharing and taking turns. Sometimes young children are asked to share their feelings in a 'What would you feel if...happened' situation so that they come to realise that other children are frightened of the dark or spiders too. Then they can realise that they are not the only one and the feeling of isolation, even guilt, can be reduced. This has to be sensitively handled by teachers who know their children so that they can offset any remarks designed to belittle or hurt. Invariably the staff act as role models for the children by using positive strategies to establish routines and acceptable ways of behaving. Careful observation allows them to boost the more vulnerable children by offering praise, and where necessary, physical support.

With slightly older children 'bullying' is often taken as a classroom topic, even before any instance of bullying has been noted. This depersonalises the issue and so encourages open discussion about incidents and the feelings of the bully and the victim when these occur. And when the stress is on the bully as an incompetent person who bullies because he/she is ineffective, then the 'glamour' of the role is questioned and the power of any potential bully may be diffused. Perhaps the bully needs positive input too so that the insecurity which causes the bullying can be rectified, although Olweus would disagree. The children would be encouraged to think through all of these issues. And so there are strategies to help. However, being unrealistic, e.g. trying to boost the victims' self-esteem by telling them they are good at something when they know full well they are not, is not helpful; in fact it could break reciprocal feelings of trust. It is better to provide them with a manageable programme of support and show them ways to cope.

There are no easy answers, but stability, routine and, whenever possible, using positive behaviour strategies can take away some of the stress. Some parents, however, have found schools unwilling or unable to make special accommodations. As a result they may decide to take their children out of school and join agencies such as Education Otherwise, but this is a huge step and many parents would not consider that they were able to cope. Perhaps parents' groups (formed to offer support for parents whose children had specific difficulties), could share strategies which they have found to 'work' and so help other people's children? Perhaps parents of children without difficulties could take time to explain the ethos of inclusion to their own children at home? Surely this kind of approach could take away some of the hurt and let all children enjoy their learning?

Movement and learning

The ABC of learning – attention, balance and control (Goddard, 1996)

Some years ago a daily radio programme of stories for very young children began by 'Uncle Mac', the presenter, asking 'Are you sitting comfortably?' and after a pause that allowed the children to adjust and squirm, he added, 'then let's begin!' As this phrase began every story session the children soon anticipated the request and wriggling to settle down and getting ready to listen became part of the fun! Looking back, one wonders if 'Uncle Mac' recognised the importance of 'sitting well' and 'being able to be still' as a prelude to learning? Very possibly it was a hidden agenda, but nonetheless it was one which was helpful to the children because it allowed them to move and then settle to concentrate on the story and enjoy it to the full! As it was a radio programme 'Uncle Mac' did not have the opportunity to observe these children to see the effectiveness of his advice. But no doubt he was hoping that there would be an adult present who was able to observe and support each child, especially when difficulties such as inappropriate restlessness or poor poise were present. Could he have known that these might just be signs of learning difficulties?

Since that time, this strategy has been recognised as a way to help learning. Teachers and other practioners have been advised to intersperse regular periods of activity with stillness times so that the length of periods of concentration that are required can be matched to the developmental level of the children's ability to stay focused. He also had some pleasant introductory music playing to establish the routine of the programme and to help develop the children's listening skills. Much more recently, teachers who have played classical music softly as background in their classrooms have called the

Mozart effect 'amazing' because it has helped to calm children and helped them stay on task.

So, knowing or not, 'Uncle Mac' was providing sound learning advice to parents and to practioners! This was to:

■ encourage children to move regularly because activity like this helps them be still and ready to listen;

■ play soft background music to calm the children and enable them to listen – music can also help to cut out any less pleasant noise that can distress noise-sensitive children;

■ give the children security by having repetition and routine – this helps develop both movement planning skills and sequencing as the children learn to anticipate and recognise the order of events.

By doing this, the learning environment should be pleasant and calm, especially for children who find concentrating difficult. Such an atmosphere is conducive to learning. It promotes an environment where the children are enabled to make good progress (DfEE, 2000) and helps them listen with enjoyment to music (SCCC, 1999).

Think back now to the aforementioned skills, i.e. being able to sit still and sit comfortably. Why are these so important? Because if the children can do these things, it is evident that that their vestibular sense (i.e. the one which controls balance) and their kinaesthetic/proprioceptive senses (the ones which help spatial orientation) are allowing them to control their bodies in movement and stillness – at least for these two skills! Moreover, if they have this control, the children are freed from having to cope with extraneous movements that distract them – and possibly others too – from being able to pay attention and concentrate on learning.

But of course sitting well (i.e. balanced and poised) and being able to sit still concern just one of the basic movement patterns, sitting. However, children must be able to carry out many patterns competently and confidently if they are to be able to participate safely and 'healthfully' at home and at school. To do this a number of competences which underlie learning must be in place. These are:

■ the ability to pay attention and not be distracted by events in the environment;

■ the ability to assimilate what is being taught;

- the ability to control the body so that gross motor, fine motor and manipulative skills are balanced and co-ordinated;

- willingness to demonstrate a (positive) change in behaviour.

Many children learn to move with enviable skill and dexterity; others 'can do' but prefer less active pursuits and a more quiescent lifestyle. An increasingly large group, however, find they are frustrated, disadvantaged and disenchanted by not being able to move well in different environments. Some of these children will catch up quite quickly if they have the correct support and regular, supervised opportunities to practise, while others will need a great deal of support and daily practice if their learning is not to be hampered by poor movement skills. The vast increase in the number of children presenting with specific learning difficulties where poor movement is a key symptom means that there are many more children who require help.

The complexity comes in that different children show different manifestations of movement problems (see Table 1.2). Some are unsure what to do. They can be seen wandering aimlessly or attempting to copy a friend. Others know but are afraid to try. Perhaps they feel overwhelmed by a large space especially if other children are milling around; perhaps they fear being hurt by the apparatus; perhaps they feel less skilled than their peers. Another group can be frustrated by knowing exactly what they need to do but can't get their bodies to obey. It is critically important that assessors identify the correct source of any difficulty and provide the correct kind of support.

Listen to a number of children explain and think what their key difficulties could be.

Table 1.2 Different aspects of movement

Having the idea Knowing what to do	Being able to move (Movement abilities/ body awareness)	Knowing where to go (Spatial orientation)
Maturation (Having the strength to cope)	Movement competence	Growth (Having the body build to cope)
Temperament (Being willing to try)	Memory (Learning from feedback)	Habituation (Transferring skill from one context to another)

CASE STUDY 1.2

Gary, age 6, explains how he feels:

'They won't let me play football because I can't score goals. I want to be in the team but no one chooses me. I'm always last to be picked. Sometimes that makes me cry, but then I get called "cry-baby." The teacher says to tell the playground supervisor and she'll make sure you get to play but it doesn't work. Most of the time I just want to go home.'

Gary has poor muscle tone in the lower half of his body. As a result of this weakness, his toes turn in. This means that any kicking action with the inside of the front of the foot propels the ball diagonally to the side instead of forwards. Running and turning corners is also difficult causing extra stress to be put on the pelvis. A programme of strengthening exercises including swimming was initiated and although improvement was quite slow it did happen.

CASE STUDY 1.3

When asked to say what he liked doing, Lewis, aged 4, replied:

'I love running and footie and I'm very good at it. I don't like painting and things like that but boys don't, do they? Not real boys anyway. I would like to do the big bricks but they fall over and bang into my legs so I don't do that any more. It would be good if I had a smaller hammer for the one that's at the building table is far too heavy for me.'

Lewis's difficulty in painting and construction came from having poor muscle tone in his shoulders and arms. He found it extremely difficult to take any weight on his arms and already, at 4 years old, he was avoiding activities he couldn't do or finding ways to compensate. When he found he could not pull himself out of a barrel (for crawling through) during outdoor play, he used his head as a lever instead. Interestingly Lewis also found crossing the midline of the body impossible. When attempting to draw a rainbow he would draw the first part of the arc then transfer the crayon to the other hand to finish. Many children with movement learning difficulties do this. It is important that this 'crossing the midline' difficulty is recognised and appropriate activities practised, for very many coping skills require two hands to do different things at the midline of the body.

Both of these children needed physiotherapy input but their teachers participated in designing their perceptual-motor programmes in school so that opportunities for strengthening work could be incorporated into the curriculum (see Chapter 5).

CASE STUDY 1.4

Mohammed, aged 8 explained:

'I like listening to stories best. I have my favourite ones and I like poetry too. I'm very good at maths for I can count up to a hundred thousand. I like jigsaws but not games outside for these horrid boys don't want to play my game any more. They always try to change bits and spoil it anyway, so I prefer to do things by myself. They want me to climb on the frame – "not likely" I said – I don't want to fall off and die. And when Jamie did fall, I shouted "told you so" and laughed!'

Mohammed's teachers found that he was changing from being a biddable, pleasant boy into an aggressive child. As a result the other children wouldn't have him for a partner. He had to be in charge of any game and if another child suggested a change, he howled with rage. He was also becoming obsessed by routine and any change of venue such as going upstairs to the painting room upset him. Close observation found that he couldn't manage the stairs, either going up or down, and so the other children passed him and he was left behind. He still used a step together pattern and preferred to hold the banister for support. Frustration with his movement skills was causing his social behaviour to deteriorate and any group learning became so fraught that he was often left to work with the classroom assistant as a partner which made him different again.

Differences in movement ability

Movement ability comes on a continuum, although children may have various placings for different types of skills. They may be able to run and jump but not write legibly, they may be able to draw with great detail but not be able to ride a bike at all. Sadly the descriptive words very often used to describe children who are not good movers (see Figure 1.4) make a hugely negative impact on their self-esteem, a state which can be extremely difficult to improve. It is much better to intervene to help before the children are even aware that a difficulty exists.

A movement continuum with commonly used descriptive words				
Nimble	Competent	Just coping	Not coping	Getting worse
Agile	Quite accurate	Clumsy	Gawky	No use at all
Dextrous		Poorly co-ordinated	Awkward	Inept
Seeks challenges	Joins in but doesn't expect to win	Gallus (Scotland)	Ungainly Slouching	Doesn't try at all Gawky
Competitive	An all-rounder	Fumbling	Butter-fingers	Blundering
Good to watch	OK in a team		No use in a team	Avoids all activity

Figure 1.4 A movement continuum with commonly used descriptive words.

Moreover, the pervasive nature of movement combined with the children's self-evaluations means that every aspect of learning can be affected. It is critically important that everyone recognises the negative effect on the children's lives if, 'I can't do' is allowed to fester and they are not helped to overcome their difficulties.

The importance of movement ability

Why is being able to move well so important? Six key reasons are summarised here.

First, just coping with the events of each day involves many movements. All the activities of daily living, e.g. speaking to communicate, getting out of bed and getting dressed, running downstairs, eating breakfast, opening cartons of juice, wiping at the toilet – these are just a few of the early morning activities which depend on dexterity, balance and co-ordination. The same sorts of demands on movement competence continue throughout every part of the day.

Second, movement underlies many if not most learning activities, e.g. controlling a pencil to write and draw, counting out materials in mathematics, pouring water, scooping sand at play or climbing on the outdoor frame. From nursery on, the school curriculum is a practical one, one that necessitates movement planning and organisation as a prelude to acting. Tasks such as collecting resources, distributing jotters and tidying up soon become part of every day. Poor movement competence therefore undermines a great deal of learning and so impacts on all aspects of development and lowers the self-esteem.

Third, without timely and constant support, self-belief flounders. Unfortunately the effect of this may transfer so the children mistakenly believe that other aspects of their development are less than competent as well. Very quickly, some become convinced that they are no use at all.

Fourth, being able to be still is generally seen as helpful in 'paying attention and concentrating on the task at hand', an essential requisite for classroom success. This requires control which depends on balance, i.e. information from the proprioceptors (nerve endings in the joints, muscles and skin) relaying spatial information which aids control. Although there may be no overt movement, the muscle groups are constantly working to sustain a position, in this case to hold the body still. Children who can't be still annoy themselves as well as the others in their class. Hence Goddard's (2002) claim that 'the ABC of learning is attention, balance and control'!

Fifth, being active contributes to the awareness of health and fitness (SCCC, 1999).Gallahue (1993) lists some important benefits of regular activity:

Increased strength and endurance, because exercise

■ *stimulates bone growth*

■ *increases bone mineralisation*

■ *reduces susceptibility to injury*

■ *enhances self-concept*

■ *enhances body image*

■ *improves lung capacity*

■ *improves circulation*

■ *improves motor performance*

■ *helps prevent injury.*

The list shows that there are many physical benefits from being active and these offer social, intellectual and emotional benefits too. For the children who can join in play activities become immersed in the play language that may involve imaginative ideas and plots. The important thing is that the language will be correct for the age group and shared colloquialisms that adults do not know can be important in gaining entry into the group. If anyone doubts this, listen to children interacting in the playground. Often they have a (shared) language quite different to that used in school.

Moreover the peer group takes an increasingly important part in establishing the children's self-esteem for young children constantly evaluate themselves according to what they perceive that others think of them. If they can be one of the group and cope with the activities the group enjoy, this is much more likely to be positive. The importance of having a favourable self-esteem is immeasurable.

Sixth, movement has been identified as a key 'faulty' component across a range of specific difficulties (Macintyre and Deponio, 2003). Many parents and teachers will recognise that poor movement competence plays a significant part in dyspraxia/developmental co-ordination disorder (DCD) and DAMP, the term more often used in Scandinavia to describe 'disorder of attention, perception and movement'. They may well be surprised, however, to see it as a contributor to dyslexia, ostensibly thinking of that as primarily a reading and spelling difficulty. But around 50 per cent of children with dyslexia display poor movement as an integral part of their condition and share the poor organisational and planning skills and the short-term memory symptoms that are found in the other specific learning difficulties (Levine, 1994).

Within ADHD (attention deficit hyperactivity disorder) too, although poor movement may not be identified first as one key 'dys' ability, it still makes an important contribution. Perhaps the fact that these children can't take time and react impulsively to any stimulation means that inept, clumsy movement may result. Alternatively their 'too quick pace' or impulsivity may detract from their planning and organisational skills, the 'other side' of movement.

What can be done? It is essential that these children have regular spells of movement interspersed with more sedentary work. This helps them stay focused. Brown and Chamove (1993) claim that 'exercise helps reduce abnormal behaviour by a third'. In effect they are saying that activity helps them be still. The Edinburgh pilot project on ADHD found that 'exercise enables pupils to take control of attentional inconsistencies' and furthermore that 'the effect of exercise lasts 60–90 minutes' (Craig, 2002). This is encouraging indeed for surely no child should be expected to be still for anything like that length of time.

It is important to recognise, however, that this kind of exercise which serves to release energy and help the children settle is fulfilling a different function from the kind which seeks to strengthen muscles or mobilise joints or help planning skills. Teachers are finding that the benefits of a regular activity break can be beneficial to all of their children, even if this is done within the confines of the classroom, but they cannot assume that this in itself is enough to reduce movement learning difficulties.

Another 'surprise' for many people comes in the claim that children with Asperger's syndrome have movement difficulties too; in fact 'these children may have co-ordination difficulties which are similar if not more extensive as the children with DCD (developmental co-ordination disorder/dyspraxia)' (Green et al., 2000).

This co-occurrence of movement incompetence across a range of learning difficulties is perhaps less obvious than the impact shown in neurological difficulties, e.g. cerebral palsy or tumour. These children need lengthy, focused specialist input. Thankfully this is usually made available. It is the children who can just cope despite having their self-esteem battered – the term is used advisedly – who have little chance of referral to these specialists. Why should this be? There are many researchers, e.g. Kaplan et al. (2001) and Goddard (2002), and paediatricians, e.g. Keen (2001) and Levine (1994), who confirm the vast increase in numbers of children presenting with specific learning difficulties that have a movement component. Yet the shortage of paediatricians and psychologists means that teachers are left – often are *required* – to make the assessments and design and carry out the remedial programmes. They may well be afraid that a 'result' which says that the child does not have a learning difficulty may deny that child specific help. Fearful of reprisals or even litigation they may decide to play safe in borderline cases (Macintyre and Deponio, 2003). On the other hand, there are a different set of implications for the teacher if the parents are upset or resentful of being told their children's progress is behind the norm even in one aspect of their development. They may even blame the teachers for not giving enough attention to their children or for not having enough specialist knowledge of each condition.

Of course the presenting number may well be an underestimation. Estimates of people with dyscalculia or difficulty understanding analogues claim that 11 per cent of the population are mathematically impaired (Dehaene and Spelke, 2003). They also explain that 'intriguingly, the precise region in the parietal lobe of the brain where this skill resides also controls finger movement'. This explains why children very often use their fingers to learn to count. Damage to this area of the brain (i.e. the intraparietal sulcus) or any underdevelopment can affect number skills.

The size of the problem

Many teachers and parents do not recognise the pervasive nature of poor movement ability and so disregard stumbles and bumps which may be the first indicators that intervention/support is required. Alternatively they may do any perplexing task for the children to save them feeling inadequate or simply to get the job done. This is a kind strategy but a mistaken one, for practice with support and guidance is the only way. And so this group of children can be denied the most effective way to progress. What sort of numbers are we talking about?

Keen (2001) claims an astounding 80 per cent increase in children presenting with difficulties but researchers have not been able to provide firm explanations to help us understand why. Many hypotheses/ideas have been posed, as dicussed in the sections which follow.

A change in many aspects of the children's lifestyles

Examples of changes in children's lifestyles include the following:

- Children do not sit at table and learn to use a knife and fork (Kirby and Drew 2002). This change denies the children practice in combining gross motor, fine motor and manipulative skills.

■ Children do not get out to play because fears of getting hurt or even of abduction cause parents to select supervised activities, e.g. ballet or judo, where the children will be taught rather than have the freedom to make up their own games. While these activities can be very helpful, they may not be individualised, i.e. at the correct level for each child. For this reason some children find 'being part of a class' stressful especially when technical demands which are beyond their capabilities are made. In these activities the children strive to reach pre-set standards and are introduced to competition. They do not have the freedom to make choices or plan things they would like to do.

■ The children's fascination with television and computer games also prevents opportunities for movement practice – the effect on their social skills and their language development as well as their poor movement is worrying many teachers, nursery nurses and health professionals.

Parental awareness and confidence

More parents are aware of symptoms, which could presage possible difficulties and are pushing for screening, diagnosis and access to programmes of early intervention.

In the past many parents were less concerned with movement competence, shrugging off 'clumsiness' as if it was just something that had to be endured. They did not appreciate the knock-on effect into other aspects of learning or the negative impact it might have on self-esteem. This new understanding raises a whole set of demands which teachers may be expected to meet without the necessary resources or even the training so to do.

As the numbers of children getting help increase, parents find out from each other how effective early intervention in movement can be and they push for support. Fewer parents are willing 'to wait and see' even if this is the advice given by their doctors. They want help and are more articulate in stating their rights. The good news is that more perceptual-motor programmes are running in (mainly primary) schools now that awareness of dyspraxia and DCD is building up.

Below are three points to consider:

■ Although there are some criteria to help diagnosis (see Appendix 4), in some specific learning difficulties, e.g. dyspraxia/developmental co-ordination disorder, there are no firm cut-off points to distinguish between those that have and those that do not have the condition. This adds to the confusion and explains why parents and children are often given conflicting advice.

■ There may be nutritional deficits that can respond to fatty acid supplementation. Stordy (1997) reports that a group of children whose motor skills were in the bottom 1 per cent of the population showed improved manual dexterity, ball skills and static and dynamic balance after twelve weeks on the course. Parents also reported a reduction in the children's dyspraxic and ADHD symptoms.

■ Today there are more caesarean births where the babies do not participate in the birth process. This means that they don't have the head turning or arm extensions which happen as they pass down the birth canal – they are 'simply' scooped out with no effort (movement) on their part. In the past they were often called 'lazy babies'. Significant research claims that this may lead to retention of primitive reflexes which then must be 'washed out' through a specific exercise programme (Goddard, 2002) if the more sophisticated postural reflexes are to take their place.

Ways to help

But of course there are children who encounter all of the aforementioned possibilities yet are nimble and skilled movers. There are other children who, despite having all the environmental advantages, find movement perplexing and unrewarding. Different children have different levels of difficulty in different aspects of their skill and this may fluctuate from day to day. They may also learn to disguise some of the difficulties they have or withdraw from experiences where their problems would become apparent. These facts combine to make accurate assessment and diagnosis very difficult.

The good news is that whatever the cause, and whatever the level of movement learning difficulty children experience, there are ways to help. Daily practice, especially if it is stress-free, can help all children move towards attaining the goals set out in the curriculum guidance documents, e.g. 'enjoy energetic activity and the feeling of well-being it brings', 'develop increasing control of fine movements of the fingers and hands' and 'engage in activities which develop hand–eye co-ordination'.

The following chapters offer ways to observe, analyse, assess then support children so that they all can have increased pleasure and competence in moving more and more competently in a range of environments. This is so that they can 'develop increasing control of fine movements of the fingers and hand', 'engage in activities which develop hand–eye coordination' and above all 'enjoy energetic activity both indoors and out and the feeling of well-being that it brings (SCCC, 1999). All of this will help them become confident in confronting all the learning challenges that will be a constant part of their lives.

CHAPTER 2

Analysing, observing and assessing movement

Analysing movement

When observing children moving, especially on large apparatus out of doors, it is often quite straightforward to identify one group of children who are particularly agile and skilled and need more challenge. Indeed they may be creative enough to make up their own games or new arrangements of apparatus to provide this. Others appear to just muddle along repeating the same sorts of things. While they are reasonably busy, they are not extending their learning in any way and not making much progress in the level of skill they display. Then there are the children who appear awkward and ungainly. They may try movements that are far beyond their capability and fall or they may persevere but not improve subsequent tries. They may not even appear to enjoy the activity at all. In each case intervention is essential to provide the best kind of support and, to find what that is, observations have to encompass a number of issues. They should be based on a structured analysis of movement properties, of physical and movement abilities and of other contextual factors such as the opportunities the children have had for previous practice. How can this be done?

Many years ago Rudolf Laban (1942) identified four movement properties for observing movement, i.e. time, weight, space and flow (see Table 2.1). These provided a structure for a detailed analysis of movement and over the years this has been used and developed to provide an invaluable assessment tool. He claimed that these key indicators would provide clues as to the exact support the children required to allow them to achieve more efficient and effective movement. A more modern version would call this process the 'how, where and when' analysis. Although all of these properties interact as the movement unfolds, they can be considered separately (analysis) and then together in the context of the whole display (synthesis). For specific sports skills, the observer would need a mental picture of the correct technique as a basis for comparing the child's performance to the mature pattern.

Table 2.2 Factors for analysis

Laban terminology	A general up-to-date framework	Linked questions
Time	When to move (quickly, slowly, in a sustained or sudden way)	Was the movement too fast or too slow at the appropriate times?
Weight	How to move (strongly, lightly)	Did the movement lack strength or use too much?
Space	Where to move How to move	Was the direction correct? Did the movement 'fit' the task?
Flow	Free flow Disconnected, abrupt movement	Was the movement pathway direct (abrupt) or flexible?

Factors for analysis

Time

The descriptive and polar words 'quick and slow', 'sudden and sustained' cover each possibility within the time sequence. Generally, the ability to move suddenly or in a controlled, sustained manner develops after quick and slow movements have been achieved. This should be noted when preparing activities for very young children.

While each child will demonstrate their basic movement patterns at their natural pace, it can be fun to try changing the pace of an action, e.g. walking quickly and as a contrast very slowly. This is so that the children can feel the effect of a change of pace on their balance and how they use the different parts of their body. In the slow walk the transfer of weight from heel to toe can be emphasised for children who tend to 'clump' the foot down and lift it again rather than rocking forward in a heel–toe action. In the quicker walk the children can be encouraged to be well poised as they take their weight onto the balls of their feet. Discussing the effect of the change of tempo can make children more aware of how they move. Using dramatic ideas can help awareness too. Some ideas could be:

■ stalking through the jungle to avoid disturbing the tigers;

■ trudging through the marshlands to get to higher land;

- skimming over the sharp shells on the beach to reach the sea;
- dragging one's feet reluctantly to meet Grandmother's friend for tea.

Weight

The descriptive words 'strong and light' cover this aspect. The child's ability to use strength appropriately, i.e. to be able to gauge how much to use at a particular moment, is very important. Think of the children who are constantly sharpening their pencils. If this is not a work-avoidance strategy, then they may not realise that, as they write, they are pressing far too hard. They are using too much strength. Children also need to be able to increase strength, i.e. to make their muscles work harder as they climb a hill or keep sitting erect for a length of time. To be able to release it at the appropriate times is important too. Letting an object go is a harder skill to acquire than grasping it. This is why children attempting to throw a ball so often find it at their feet instead of seeing it soar through the air. Their hands have not been able to release the ball at the correct time. They have grasped the ball too hard and for too long. They have to learn to control the amount of strength they use.

Space

There are two aspects to 'space'. The first is space 'where', the second space 'how'.

Space where

'Space where' is really directionality. If children understand the space words forwards, backwards, over, under and through, below and beyond and later diagonally, and have opportunities to move according to these directions, they will gradually develop skill in moving directly, i.e. efficiently with no waste of time or energy, to the correct place. Learning to write will also be helped. This is because scribing the letters needs a basic understanding of directions, e.g. 'start at the top, move down...' Mathematical calculations such as subtraction also depend on directional understanding (for details see Chapter 4) as do map reading skills or the everyday task of finding one's way around town.

Many children have little awareness of 'behind' and seem unable to feel their backs or have their backs initiate movements. Apparatus such as the spinning cone give lots of fun and encourage the children to recognise the impact the large muscles in the back can make to strong movement. Sometimes the proprioceptors in the back can be slow to relay positional information so that actions such as sitting down or lining up with other children can be poorly cued. They need lots of fun activities to help them develop this perceptual skill. Old-fashioned singing games, e.g. 'In and out the dusty bluebells', or a modern version of 'I sent a letter to my love' where the children stand behind one another doing 'pitter pitter patter on my shoulder', could very usefully be revived!

Distance

Once the direction is understood, then the distance dimension has to be considered. Can the children make spatial decisions that tell them how far they wish to travel? Can they appreciate whether their bodies will fit into a certain space? If not, they are likely to run into walls or fall off kerbs into the road, bump into other children as they play or drop articles that were supposed to be placed safely on tables. In the past these children would have been called the clumsy ones, a negative term that has now been jettisoned because it suggested that it was the children's fault when a specific learning difficulty could be the cause.

Space how

This aspect concerns how the children move in space, i.e. whether they move directly or take a meandering pathway. Very often children who need a great deal of space, perhaps stretching out their arms as they walk or run, are compensating for having a poor sense of balance. Overweight children too often move in a 'galumphing' fashion that tends to involve barging and bumping. This may be because their thighs are so rounded that they rub as they pass! On the other hand, finely built children can use too little space. They often adopt a narrow posture that makes them appear afraid to venture out into space and indeed they may find large spaces threatening. They seem to feel more secure staying small and being in a confined space. Their kinesthetic sense may not be giving them sufficient help in orientating themselves. Observers can be easily confused into thinking the skill such as running and jumping is poor, when indeed it is 'coping with space' that is causing the problem.

Flow

Movement flows when the separate parts come together with no hiatus or interruption. In flowing movement that is so pleasing to the eye, the correct selection of time, weight and space has been achieved. This aids the pace or momentum of the action which is then controlled in the recovery phase. When all of this occurs, progression into a subsequent attempt is smooth and the movement appears easy.

Transitions

Laban also explained that every action could be broken down into three parts. These were the preparation, the action and the recovery. In the transitions or the moments between the preparation, the action and the recovery phases of the action, the body has to make the necessary adjustments so that the natural rhythm of the whole movement is not broken. When any movement is practised and repeated, the recovery phase should blend into the preparatory phase of the next attempt. This allows one part to flow into the next, preserving energy and making the movement both effective and efficient. Laban pointed out that even when the discrete parts were competently done, poor transitions could spoil the process and the outcome. This means that analysing the transition(s) must be part of assessing the whole. Very often the transition happens quickly, yet when there are difficulties, it can be the stumbling block. A sequence of movement would involve:

preparation · transition · action · transition · recovery · transition · preparation

Analysing each part of the movement while retaining the picture of the whole is necessary if support/teaching is to be targeted correctly. The second transition should be using feedback from the first try to adapt the second. Many children appear unable to do this.

Note. Before recording assessments it is a good idea to check the children's footwear! If shoes or trainers have to be worn, the soles should not be rigid as this prevents the transfer of the body weight from heel to toe, i.e. the rocking action which helps propulsion forward. It goes without saying that resources such as hard balls should not intimidate and that the children should be clear about what they are aiming to do. Nor should they be stressed by having to do anything in a hurry.

Movement, of course, is a combination of all these aspects. The skilled mover makes intricate movements seem effortless. With sustained practice, high-level performers 'get it right'. When they don't, their coaches will analyse their patterns just as teachers and parents must do for children in the early years.

Example 1

A child running up to jump over a rope that has been placed on two skittles

Preparation: The approach run

The approach run must be fast enough to allow enough momentum to be built up to take the child into the jump. If it is too slow, the effort required to make the jump is vastly increased and the child may not gain enough height or not attempt the jump at all. If the run-up is too fast, the child will overshoot the point of take off and run through the rope. Recognising the point for take-off is a spatial decision that the children need to practise. This is why it is not a good idea to have children jumping over canes, for misjudgements (timing, spatial) can result in them jumping on top of the cane that may snap causing injury.

Action: The jump

The child must have developed foot dominance to be sure of the take-off foot. This is an important point for assessment, for after a little time to practise, children should have a definite preference. If they continue to 'fumble with their feet' the action will not become efficient and flowing. Asking the children to 'feel which foot gives the strongest jump' in a series of trial turns often helps them decide. During the jump the body should stay balanced, not swerve to one side. If it does, the rope should be lowered so that the amount of effort required to take the body into the air is reduced. The strength in the arm action also needs to be observed as children will often over-use their dominant arm to help lift their bodies and in so doing upset the balance of the action.

Recovery: The landing

The landing should be resilient, i.e. the knees and ankles bending to absorb the weight and prevent any jarring. The body weight should be balanced so that the trunk stays upright. Any untoward forward lean could result in tipping forward, possibly falling. There must also be enough leg strength to push back to the upright position ready to run again. The body weight then travels forward onto the toes to aid propulsion.

In the landing phase, the weight has to be absorbed by resilient knee and ankle work that then pushes the body erect again. If the legs stay too strong, the landing will be jerky and the body will be pushed forward into overbalancing. On the other hand if the legs lack strength they may collapse. Until the children have mastered landing with control, they should not be allowed to jump from heights.

(a) Jumping off the bench

(b) Landing in a well-balanced position

During the second year of a daily perceptual-motor programme, Mitchell has learned to control his landing from the low bench. He explains that he has 'developed springs in his knees,' and his teacher is assured that he will be able to cope with landings from different heights and directions. This is essential for safety.

Example 2

Catching a ball (underarm throw)

Children usually learn to catch a ball before they get involved in the other ball skills such as kicking or aiming or hitting or scoring goals. The same battery of competences is required, however, and the skills can be analysed in the same way.

Preparation

The children must be able to track the incoming ball and move their hands and feet at the correct time to make the catch. If they clasp too quickly, the ball hits their hands; if they clasp too slowly the ball flies past. Children who find this difficult may be field dependent, i.e. they may not see the ball emerge from the background until it is too late to make the necessary adjustments. Using a brightly coloured ball and ensuring that the children are not looking into strong light can help this difficulty. Substituting a balloon (with rice inside if there is a hearing impairment) can mean there is more time for the child to track and appreciate the rhythm of the move. Throws should be sympathetic until the rhythm of the throw/catch is mastered. Thereafter distances and directions can be adjusted to suit the children's increasing competence.

Action

When the children do manage to grasp the ball, they have to apply the correct amount of strength: too little and the ball slips from their grasp; too much and they have difficulty releasing the ball to throw it back. Spatial decisions are important too. If the hands are held too far apart then the timing of the action will be affected. And ideally the catcher must be balanced so that the position of the body can be readily adjusted to make the catch if the throw is beyond their immediate reach.

Recovery

In the third phase, as the ball is caught the body probably moves back to absorb the catch and then recoils to regain a balanced stance or to add strength to the next throw. If the feet stay square on in the catch they need to move to the diagonal position to allow the arm to pass alongside the body to instigate the throw.

The flow within the movement is most easily seen when one arm sweeps back and then moves smoothly into the throw. The back swing can be free flowing and gather strength if the foot opposite to the hand is forward, with the arm on that same side outstretched to aid balance.

Example 3

A comparative analysis

An analysis of an immature kicking pattern contrasting with a practised, mature one follows. The first is by a young child, the second by a skilled adult taking a penalty kick. The key aim for both is to score a goal.

The child

The child is likely to choose a standing start and the ball will be still. He will use an immature kicking pattern.

▶

Preparatory phase: The child

a) checks the position of the goal mouth

b) approaches the ball and selects the kicking foot.

Transition 1: The child, standing still beside the ball,

a) adjusts his weight to free that foot

b) uses the opposing arm to help balance

c) summons up as much strength as possible.

Action: The child

a) swings his leg back and then forward to the point of impact

b) hits the ball with his toe

c) leans back to compensate for over-extension of the kicking leg.

Transition 2: The child

a) transfers his weight back onto two feet

b) regains the upright position.

Recovery phase: The child watches where the ball goes, runs to retrieve it, then carries it back.

The adult

The more experienced adult (who also has longer limbs and more strength and who can reflect on previous attempts and use feedback from these to inform this attempt) uses a mature pattern.

Preparatory phase: The adult builds a mental image of the kick that will be successful, considers the distance, direction and speed of the kick, decides where in the goal mouth he should aim for and notes the position of the defence.

Transition 1: The adult will balance the weight on the balls of the feet, lean slightly forward to balance the leg action, glance at the goalmouth and recheck the position of the ball, and select the distance and direction of the approach run.

Action: The adult

a) will use a fast step pattern gauging the strength, speed and direction required

b) kick the ball with the inside of the front of the foot

c) lean slightly back at the moment of impact

d) keep the head up to check where the ball has gone.

Transition 2: The adult

a) will quickly adjust his weight forwards to regain balance

b) reorganise his feet to begin running.

Recovery: The adult will

a) evaluate the result and decide on adjustments needed in a next attempt

b) use the momentum of the kicking action to propel him into the run or lean back so that the stance acts as a brake on the momentum of the kicking action.

Each part of the action is important and when children experience difficulties, breaking down the pattern into its component parts is essential. Perhaps at the start the child has not thought through what is required? In that case a 'stop and think' suggestion should be made. But what has the child to think about?

Some questions for analysis
_____

Time errors

■ Did the child rush into the action and become flustered? If yes, then slowing each part and explaining where the 'fast, strong part' should come needs to happen.

■ Was each part too slow so that momentum did not build up? If yes, then a faster approach possibly over a shorter distance would help.

▶

Weight errors

- Was the weight carried on the balls of the feet or was the body weight held back over the heels? If so, the kick would not propel the ball forward effectively.

- Did the child use too much strength and overbalance at the point of impact? Or perhaps more strength was required and the distance of the kicker from the ball needs to be reconsidered?

From these descriptions it can be seen that the skilful completion of any movement task depends on a number of underlying abilities. Accurate perception is very important too and is covered in Chapter 3.

Movement abilities

Once the structure of a movement is considered the next step – or more realistically the concurrent step – is to consider the movement abilities, i.e. to appreciate if the children have developed 'what it takes' to allow them to be competent in their attempts. These movement abilities are balance, rhythm, co-ordination and body awareness (including body boundary).

Balance

Balance is not just a competence required by trapeze artists in the circus – it is the central component of efficient movement. A balanced movement means that there is no extraneous flailing of arms or legs; the movement is poised and effective. All movements, even everyday occurrences such as standing up and sitting down require balance if the movement is to be done without stumbling. In a similar vein, being still requires balance too. This is why there are two descriptors, i.e. dynamic balance and static balance. Most people would associate balance with being still and not realise its importance in maintaining equilibrium as the body moves.

Children who are constantly on the move, i.e. those who can't sit or stand still, may be moving to energise their vestibular system (see Chapter 3). They are seeking more information to tell them where they are functioning in space. This is necessary if they are to have security and confidence. Without it they may rock or race around. They are often told to 'be still' when it is well nigh impossible for them to comply.

Lucy is learning about balance.

Jacqui and Alana are helping each other to experiment with balancing positions on the duck board.

Adults can help children to feel a balanced position by intervening, usually slowing the children's movement down, 'Wait a moment and feel your balance' (checking that the child understands how to sustain a poised starting position) can be enough to alert the child's kinaesthetic sense. Many children need constant reminders as they sit to write, stand to pull trousers on or stretch to catch a ball. Lessons in the classroom, e.g. on symmetry, can include the children trying out 'different positions of the body' and deciding whether they are symmetrical. In this fun way, they can then appreciate how the different positions of their body parts can affect their balance.

Josh, as may be deduced from his headband, is a reindeer. He is keeping balanced in a safe position.

In any work on apparatus it is important that adults analyse the 'balance demands' of different arrangements so that children with a poor sense of balance have safe opportunities to practise and develop their skill.

Rhythm

Every movement has an intrinsic rhythm. Walking smartly has a regular beat that provides momentum and so saves energy. Climbing stairs, as just one example, is much more time- and energy-efficient if a rhythmical pace is used. Most activities of course have changing rhythmic patterns as they unfold and much of the fun and satisfaction comes through mastering the change. Think of children approaching the chute in the swing park. They don't walk – they run and control their speed as they reach the ladder. The climb is then fairly slow as children clutch the handrail and thump too hard on each step, but this is followed by a swoop down the chute. The change of pace adds spice to the activity. Moving from standing to sitting or lying at the top of the steps is a nice example of how a transition can be the trickiest part of the movement.

If children have difficulties in moving efficiently making them aware of the rhythm they use and the more effective rhythm can be very helpful. Adults can accompany their movement by sounds or words, e.g. 'run and run and ready to jump' till the children are able to do this for themselves.

Children with dyslexia are often unable to detect the beats within words and this may hinder their acquisition of speech patterns and later their reading (as the meaning may be altered by the rhythm which in turn impacts on comprehension). The finding that some children don't respond to a rhythmical breakdown/accompaniment can be an early indication of dyspraxia and suggest that a great deal of listening and moving to sounds could be a vital intervention.

Co-ordination

Co-ordination is needed whenever different parts of the body are required to work in harmony to complete a task. For gross motor skills to be effective, whole-body co-ordination can be required. Children who have poor body awareness or sense of where their body parts are functioning in the space around them will have difficulty making them work together at the correct time. They need activities that will develop their body awareness (see Chapter 5) and very often their sense of timing too. Sometimes it is possible to reduce the co-ordination demands by having the children sit instead of standing, e.g. in painting. Sometimes the environmental demands can be reduced so that the activity is learned as a closed skill rather than an open one.

Some skills require hand–eye co-ordination, e.g. aiming at a target or threading beads. Others need co-ordination of eyes and feet, e.g. in dribbling a ball or getting onto an escalator. In advanced skills such as skiing or driving, all the different kinds are required at once. This explains why they are so difficult to achieve!

Body awareness: body boundary

To be able to move with precision and efficiency, children must be able to feel where the different parts of their body are in relation to each other and where they are functioning in the environment in which they move. This includes being sure of where they end and the outside world begins. Many children are unsure of the position of their elbows and ankles and shoulders and most seem totally unaware of their backs. These deficiencies cause movement to be clumsy and awkward, because if they don't recognise where the parts are, how can they obey instructions such as 'shrug your shoulders' or even 'put your hand up'!

Even when there are no obvious difficulties, practioners should determine whether the children are depending heavily on their vision rather than their proprioceptive (feeling) sense on which body awareness depends. If the children are over-dependent on their visual perception they will take a

Jake enjoys making the spinning cone turn. As the arms and back initiate the action, this activity helps awareness of the back. Jake's protruding leg shows that work on awareness of the legs and feet needs to takes place too. Imagine the effect on his ability to walk, run and jump if he cannot tell where his feet are. Cycling and kicking a ball will be affected too.

moment to look and check rather than moving the limbs immediately. Then when their vision is required for other things, movements may be clumsy and inaccurate. This is because of the inadequacy of the feedback they receive from their proprioceptors that should alert them to where they are functioning in the space around them.

A poor sense of body boundary means that children are unsure of where they end and the outside world begins. The most obvious effects are seen in fumbled grasping actions and an inability to release the fingers when they are required to let go. This affects gross motor skills too. If the children have to look to see where their chair is and check its position in relation to other objects, rather than sensing its position in relation to their hips and thighs, then there is a moment's delay. Repeated, this can cause the child to be 'always last' and, in a harsh environment, the object of scorn.

Playing 'Simon says' kinds of games, especially if the children play with their eyes closed, can develop a sense of body awareness. This can be very illuminating, immediately revealing those who do not know!

Open and closed skills

When children find movement difficult it is often helpful to change an open skill into a closed skill. This means reducing the environmental demands until the basic technique is mastered and then gradually (if possible) reintroducing them. Examples could include the following:

- *Learning to swim in the warm, calm water of a swimming pool.* In this situation, with few other swimmers to make waves, balance is much easier than when sea waves and ghastly mouthfuls of cold salt water make the children struggle to hold their heads out of the water. (Even skilled competitive swimmers swimming in lanes could be said to be using closed skills as they are minimally affected by the environment. This changes in actual competitions when the pace of the strokes has to be altered according to the skill of the competitors but the external demands are still less than swimming in the sea!)

- *Getting dressed.* Many children find the organisation and planning inherent in this activity very difficult. If this can be reduced by using charts to indicate the order of donning garments then the children's attention can be focused on the intricate movements (which require co-ordination and balance) needed to put on trousers and do up zips.

It is important to simplify the underlying demands of movements so that they can be achieved. Then, as confidence and competence is gained, the visual help can be reduced. Analysing what is involved when a child has difficulties can lead to removing the stress and this is a sure way to enhance learning.

Observing and assessing movement

Assessment

Observation and assessment are inextricably linked, but as there are different ways of doing both, there are many considerations that should come into force before any conclusions about children's movement competence are drawn. Decisions about whether to use a standardised test to 'measure' competence, e.g. the ABC test of motor competence, or whether informed assessments drawn from a variety of sources such as parents, teachers, nursery nurses and health professionals would produce more widespread evidence are important. Such decisions might depend on the suitability of the standardised test, for example, does it measure the kinds of competencies which are causing concern, and even if this is the case, are the test items appropriate for the age and stage of the particular child? And if 'other sources' are chosen, do all the observers have the eyes that can see and are they able to be unbiased in their judgements?

Assessing movement which is transitory, requires experience and a sound understanding of what is to be observed. These sorts of procedures and decisions would be especially critical if the result could mean labelling the children or if they were to be used to plan a specific activity programme. And following observations, analysis must probe all the possible reasons why the children's movement is as it is, for it may be that poor self-esteem or retained primitive reflexes or even inhibitions or dietary deficiencies are not allowing the acquisition of more mature movement patterning.

Assessments have different purposes and different techniques. These will be considered in turn.

Summative assessment

Assessment at the end of a period of input/support is useful in that it provides information as to how well the children have adapted to and succeeded in a particular programme. This summary information (based on the product of the exercise) can be communicated to parents or passed on to new teachers so that they know what has been achieved and what competencies still need support. The downside of this is that the information is usually communicated too late to act as a vehicle for intervention and ongoing support. This is the information gathered for monitoring targets or levels of achievement. Often the results are used with others to compare the performance of a group or a school in relation to similar groups. They can also be used for league tables and for informing policy-makers, e.g. to show how newly included children are faring in the mainstream school.

Formative/diagnostic assessment

As its name suggests, this form of assessment analyses the process of learning, i.e. the ongoing demonstration of the children's competence as a piece of teaching unfolds or as opportunities to be creative or innovative or more skilled in any competence arise. This means that timely adjustments can be made in the pace of teaching, the level of expectation for individual children and the amount of support that is given. This could take the form of reinforcement work, extension work or providing resources that allow more hands-on practice. The rationale is that children are assessed through having their work continually evaluated and the outcome adjusted so that they do not fail or so that they are stretched to fulfil their potential. This information is gathered for personal profiles or the compilation of IEPs (individual education plans). The strength of this kind of assessment is that observations can be made in different settings and that everyday coping skills can form part of the record. Aspects of personal and social development can also be included, e.g. how well the children interact in a group or whether they approach new tasks confidently or with trepidation or whether they are willing to do them at all. This is possible, as the report is usually detailed as a checklist or in writing rather than giving a score.

This explanation shows how the two types of assessment have a different purpose. It also raises the question as to how assessment should be handled if it is not to cause unnecessary stress, especially for young children. There are important questions here.

■ Should the children be aware that assessment is taking place? Even if knowing causes stress, is there a moral imperative that says that children should know what is happening?

■ Or if knowing about the assessment changes the children's behaviour, are the results biased or made more accurate by the change?

■ Should assessments be done in different contexts to give a full picture of each child's competence? If so, how are competencies such as creativity or imagination to be monitored? Does storytelling cover these or does the wider spectrum of possibilities, e.g. role-play, need to be considered? Perhaps the criteria for assessment need to be set out so that the parameters of the assessment are made clear.

Any assessment report must only consider the competencies that were observed and assessed. The danger is that false assumptions can easily be made, for example that because the children can do/cannot do one activity, another will necessarily be proficient/deficient.

For many years, teachers believed that if children's gross motor patterns were sound, their fine motor skills would be competent too. They would just appear later in the developmental time frame. Newer research, however, claims that this is not so (Stein, 2000). There are many children who can climb and run or run and jump who cannot write legibly. Conversely there are those who can write a beautiful script yet find it impossible to crawl or combine gross motor patterns with any kind of confidence. Yet given the earlier stance, it is not difficult to see how assessors could mistakenly accept this transfer of skills as a probability when the different timing of neurological 'wirings' prevents this happening.

Making prognoses from assessments should also be avoided. Especially in very young children, it is difficult to estimate how maturation will affect progress. This is because many variables, e.g. the children's temperament, their general health, the kind and amount of support they receive at home and at school, can impinge and cause unexpected boosts or disappointments. It is better to stay with results as they are at that moment in time and compare those with the ones that come later. Assuring parents and teachers that a child 'will soon be able to do' a certain skill can lead to 'but you said' type of recriminations when this is not achieved, quite apart from the disappointment for all concerned. On the other hand, everyone has to be reassured that regular, sustained, carefully taught practice will result in progress.

Criterion-referenced and grade-related criterion assessment

Another two kinds of assessment influence the kind of observational techniques that should be employed. In criterion-referenced assessment a number of criteria are set out and the assessment only considers these points (see Figure 2.1). The results are recorded 'Yes' or 'No', meaning that the child can or cannot do the task. A more complex form may ask the observer to grade the performance, sometimes using an A,B,C or 1, 2, 3 format. At other times terms like 'shows some difficulty' or 'has severe difficulty' may be used. This becomes known as a grade-related criterion assessment. The danger is that cumulating scores (which often assessors try to do for convenience and brevity) just doesn't make sense. Adding together the score taken from the ability to catch a ball with the one that was given for writing has only, at best, a tenuous connection. It makes no more sense than adding apples and oranges.

Criterion-referenced profile		
Please complete the following profile for Jude. Please tick the appropriate boxes.		
Name: Demi **Date:** 14.10.03	**Yes, can do**	**No, cannot do**
Can crawl		*
Can stand and sit still	*	
Can pick up small objects using the pincer grip		*
Can hold a paint brush comfortably	*	
Can climb on the frame		*
Can cope independently at the toilet		*
Can balance on a wide bench	*	
Can control a pencil		*

Figure 2.1 Criterion-referenced profile.

The point of criterion-referenced assessment, graded or not, is that the observers are seeking to identify specific things. They know in advance exactly what they are looking for. Sometimes they record incidence, e.g. how many times the observed child was off task in the allocated time span. While these recordings should ensure accuracy for these particular competencies, some important happenings may be missed.

Another possibility is when observers set out with a blank slate and record exactly what the child does within a certain length of time. In the Nursery, teachers and nursery nurses use sticky labels to make quick notes (see Figure 2.2). Sometimes 'what the child chooses to do or chooses to avoid' can be discerned by recording on a time sampling framework, examples of which are shown in Figures 2.3 and 2.4. Both fit with other observations to build a picture of a child's particpation.

> 28.11.03
>
> Jill avoids going near the climbing frame. She won't attempt the low approach plank. She can manage steps indoors so climbing may be alright. She stands and watches her friend climbing but won't be encouraged to try.
>
> * Check Jill's hand and finger stength

Figure 2.2 Sticky label recording.

Name: Sean aged 4.8 (second year in Nursery)	**Observation no.** 8 this term
Time	**Observed activity**
9.00	Reluctantly sits down – pushes his way to the front of the group
9.01	Turns and hits the boy behind then bursts into tears
9.05	Sits beside the teacher to sing 'Good morning to everyone' jingle
9.07	Won't relax – shoulders very tense. Asks 'When can I go outside?'
9.08	Teacher asks him to sit quietly for a moment more. He struggles up and runs across the room. He bangs into a table and yells out about his sore leg.
9.10	He has hauled his coat off the peg and is heading for the door.

Figure 2.3 Example of time sampling (1).
Such a ten-minute observation gives a detailed picture of events. The times are not decided beforehand but are noted to provide a time sequence.

At other times proficiency in a particular competence or clearly articulated speech or whatever arises that is relevant to the child can be the key factor. Later, a bank of these observations – often made by different people – is studied so that a picture of the child's involvement emerges. From these different kinds of recordings, information is pulled together so that subsequent interventions can be focused on specific areas of need.

Planned time every 5 mins:	Child: Lucy Observation to gather activities chosen and avoided outdoors
14.0	Selects doll and pram and wanders round the outside of the apparatus area.
14.5	Approaches the bench and holds the sides but doesn't climb on.
14.10	Jackie approaches and they go to the wendy house together.
14.15	Both come out. Jackie is shouting and Lucy runs quietly behind her.
14.20	Jackie helps to steady Lucy as she walks along the bench.
14.25	Lucy looks very pleased but refuses Jackie's plea to try again.
14.30	Back to the doll and pram now, but this time goes nearer the apparatus to watch and looks as if she could be tempted to join in.

Figure 2.4 Example of time sampling (2). This observation is to monitor what the child chooses to do and avoids doing.

Observation

Using video as an observational tool

The transitory nature of movement makes observation difficult. It is over in a flash and needs practised eyes to 'see' what is afoot. Often new observers have no doubt that 'something is wrong'. But being able to identify what it is, is another story.

Video recordings of children's movement are a major source of information. They can be replayed with different viewers and observations can be compared. Often many repeated viewings still give surprises. Before viewing it is a good idea to list the things that are to be spotted, e.g. delay in responding, poor balance, hypotonia (low muscle tone), or else the shot can be over and extraneous things can divert attention away from the key points which should be in focus. However, there should always be room for observations that pick up new points.

Sometimes teachers worry that the video will not give a true picture of the children's movement. 'If they know they are being filmed,' they say, 'they will do things a whole lot better.' This is interesting because it throws up the point that children who can do things better and who normally don't bother or who are in too much of a rush need a different kind of intervention to those who cannot improve their performance. This is a subtly different reason for filming. This video is not to get a general picture of events that might be the case if, for example, social interaction in group work was to be the focus. It is to discover what is wrong – a 'what' that is not down to carelessness or lack of practice, but some kind of real deficit.

Of course another way to mitigate this worry would be to make filming a usual part of the day, for young children just love to see themselves on the screen. The youngest ones are likely to watch themselves and not compare their aptitude to that of other children, but this point would need to be considered in using replays for the older ones. Of course filming the children has to be checked out with every parent and written permission gained. Often it is easiest to issue a form that both parents just have to sign. Reassurances about the film being kept in school and used for observations only should be made. This is vitally important and arrangements for parents with English as an additional language have to be put in place.

(For further guidance on research techniques see 'Macintyre, 2001'.)

Examples of the process of assessment

Table 2.2 Assessing a fine motor/manipulative skill

Activity	Points for assessment	Additional points
Doing a jigsaw (fine motor / manipulative skill)	Does the child: ■ Use the picture on the box as a guide? If so, how often does the child refer to the picture? ■ Consider how the shapes fit together? Use colour recognition to help? Can the child: ■ Manipulate two hands at the midline of the body? ■ Use the pincer grip? ■ Place the pieces accurately? ■ Let go?	How long does the child persevere? Is isolation a danger? Is tracking from the box to the table an issue? Is the same puzzle always selected? What is the child's posture like, e.g. poised, slumping or constantly shifting? Which is the dominant hand? Are two hands used equally or is one hidden away? Is there any tremor? What is the child's reaction if another child wants to help? Does the child show pleasure and a sense of achievement when the puzzle is complete?

No matter which data collection method is used, the crux of the matter is that observers appreciate why assessments are made. A number of questions can help the subtleties of assessment and the comprehensive nature of the information that can result to be understood. Some examples are given in Tables 2.2 to 2.6.

Table 2.3 Assessing a gross motor skill

Activity	Points for assessment	Additional points
Climbing stairs (gross motor skill)	Does the child use a step together pattern on each step? Is the child sure of the leading foot? Does the child look for extra support e.g. clutching the banister? Can the child make the transitions, i.e. getting onto the first step and off the top one smoothly?	Is the correct amount of strength and speed used – or does the child use too much momentum, which leads to being off-balance? Is the stride pattern sure or does the child 'ditter'? Does the child have to concentrate hard to plan the movement? Is the child well poised or is watching the feet necessary? Are the shoulders tense? Can the child carry a toy or book upstairs without undue hassle, e.g. losing balance?
Returning downstairs	Is the child fazed by looking out into space? Is a step together pattern used here when the more mature pattern was evident in climbing? Does the child lean back away from the direction of travel – or too far forward? At the foot of the stair can the child adapt to a walking or running pattern without stopping?	Does the child slide down on the tummy? If so can the body be manoeuvred easily into that position? Is the action smooth or stilted? Are the transitions from the climbing- down pattern made easily or does the child stumble and fall over?

Table 2.4 Assessing a manipulative skill

Activity	Points for assessment	Additional points
Writing (manipulative/fine motor skill)	Does the child sit well balanced or tend to slouch over the page? Is the pencil held so that smooth writing is possible? Is the pencil sharp enough /too sharp / too easily broken / thick barrelled? Can the child manage better with lined paper that helps spatial decisions? Is tracking from the board difficult? Does the child have enough room? Does the child understand the task? Is the child motivated by the task?	Check that the feet are supported and that the desk height is suitable. Many pencil grips are available apart from the rubber, triangular one. Left-handed pens are available for left-handed children. Marking 'where to begin' can help children get started. Provide a copy of the work alongside the child. A left-handed child alongside a right-handed one may be cramped Can the task be broken down into smaller fragments to allow success? Is it possible to give the child a choice to stimulate enthusiasm?

It can be seen then that each assessment holds the potential for considering all aspects of development:

- *intellectual* – or the planning and organising part of movement including 'knowing what to do';

- *social* – or the co-operative part of movement which helps children work together to accomplish a task or solve a problem;

- *perceptual-motor* – or the part which takes cues from the environment and uses them to carry out the actions;

- *emotional* – or the part that temperament and attitude plays in allowing children to participate.

Table 2.5 Assessing an oral skill

Activity	Points for assessment	Additional points
Speaking to communicate (fine motor oral skill)	Can the child articulate clearly? Has the child the words to communicate? Does the child understand what is being said? Can the child hold eye contact during the interaction – or is this consciously avoided? Does the child understand turn-taking? Does the child wait to hear what others say? Does the child shout out or intervene inappropriately?	If not, can the parents understand? Can other children understand? Is this a language rather than a speech deficit? Is comprehension a problem generally or with one person only? Does the child stare into space or do the eyes flicker? (If so specialist help is required.) Play games such as peep-boo to establish the 'rules.' Can the child be persuaded to stay to listen? Does the child empathise with what others say / feel and respond appropriately?

Table 2.6 Assessing a complex motor skill

Activity	Points for assessment	Additional points
Catching a ball* (Manipulative/ gross motor skill)	Does the child prepare to make a catch? Does the child shy away as the ball approaches? Does the child attempt to catch but make the action too late and only clutch thin air?	Does the child recognise the trajectory of the approaching ball? The child may not have seen the ball till it is too late to position correctly. Use a balloon filled with rice instead. Speak the action – ready, watch, catch – to help the timing of the action. Begin by having gentle throws into an outstretched basket and gradually increase the distance and speed of the throw.

*N.B. Some children are afraid of being hurt by a hard ball and will take part willingly when a smaller, softer ball is substituted.

These interacting aspects of development are shown in Figure 2.5.

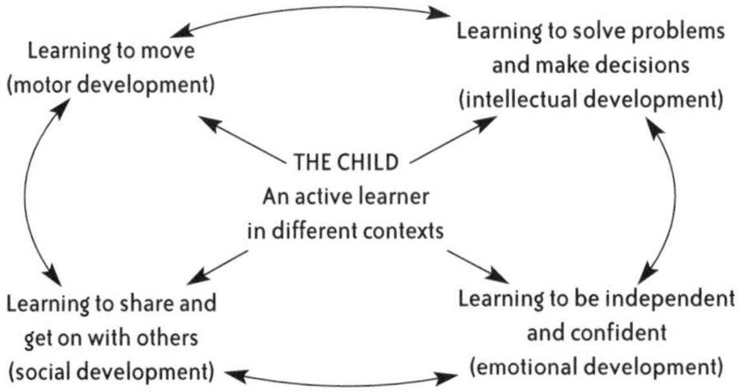

Figure 2.5 Different aspects of development.

The fact that these developmental processes do interact means that it could be inappropriate to consider each in isolation. Achieving movement skills has an immediate effect on the children's self-esteem, which may in turn enable them to tackle other learning tasks with increased confidence. Being able to ride a bike – as just one example – allows children to go off with their friends and so they can explore new territory. This develops both their social skills and their ability to be independent. This is an added bonus to achieving the movement skills themselves.

An implicit part of movement learning means that as a skill is acquired, the children learn about the intellectual side of movement. They learn about control, co-ordination, balance and spatial orientation. They also learn how to make the planning and organisational judgements that will bring each of the movement abilities into play at the correct time.

Other factors in assessment

The sections above have considered assessment as a general concept. There are other factors which must also be considered if assessments are to be personal and meaningful to the children and their parents.

Chronological age

Obviously the age of the children influences what they can be expected to do. To give assessors guidance, researchers have developed tables of 'norms' (see Appendix 1). These, within a fairly wide range, give a rough guide as to what children of different ages should be able to do. If the children vary markedly from this or parents find there are skills the children cannot do, e.g. crawling, then some support from a health professional could be invaluable in reassuring the parents or suggesting early strategies to help.

Body build

Children will inherit a particular build, which may influence their choice of activities. Finely built children may prefer non-contact games because they have not the weight or the strength to compete. Children who are overweight may find exercise makes them uncomfortably aware of their size and this restricts what they want to do. For these reasons, body build should be sympathetically considered in planning programmes for children. Different resources, e.g. benches of different heights, can provide appropriate levels of challenges for balancing skills while lighter equipment, e.g. table tennis bats and balls, can help develop movement abilities without causing the kind of apprehension, even hurt, which could arise if footballs were used.

So, while assessing, it is important not to confuse the effects of body build with 'inability to do'. Heavily built children are likely to use too much momentum to overcome their body weight. This causes overbalancing and an appearance of being clumsy. It is the weight factor that needs attention rather than the movement skill itself. On the other hand, fragile children may avoid activities, not because they have not the movement skills to do them well, but because they are fearful of the crowd or the wide-open space or the rumbustious behaviour of other children.

Maturation

Perhaps the most fundamental influence on movement competence is maturation. Often the two terms, growth and maturation, are used interchangeably, but essentially they are different. Maturation is the term used to describe the inbuilt sequences of changes, e.g. walking, that determine progress. These happen without teaching. Children cannot walk until they are 'ready', i.e. they have the neurological and physical development to allow that to happen. This is why assessors are reluctant to record 'can't do decisions' if there is the possibility that they could be overtaken by maturation. Especially in borderline cases, awareness of the mitigating effects of maturation may cause practioners to 'wait and see.'

Intellectual competence

Many highly intelligent children are skilled movers but others, equally intelligent, are not. They often show a discrepancy between their 'intellectual IQ' and their 'performance IQ'. In addition, of course, there are many children with global developmental delay, which means they are achieving less than their peer group right across the spectrum of competences. What intellectual factors could contribute to poor movement? Among such factors are:

- a poor short-term memory;

- inability to habituate movement patterns, i.e. to do them automatically with little conscious planning;

- distractibility or difficulty in attending;

- poor communication skills.

The short-term memory – or working memory as it is often called – makes a significant contribution to children's progress. Those who find it extremely difficult, even impossible, to remember need many over-learning opportunities. Ideally these should be with a patient teacher who understands that questions such as 'What did we do this morning?' can be met by a blank look. At home and in school it is understandable when frustration elicits comments such as 'But you must know this, you did it yesterday.' However, these responses are self-defeating, only fuelling the children's feelings of inadequacy. Such children need strategies to help them remember such as timetables, prompt cards and routines that give security. Breaks in routine can be frightening for children who cannot remember similar experiences and know that they survived/enjoyed them.

Environment

Development always depends on both inherited and acquired factors; the latter critically influenced by the context or environment in which the children grow and learn. No one can really say how that influences the children's movement prowess unless the children's diet influences their strength or if lack of practice is so severe that the children fail to catch up when compensatory resources and opportunities are provided. This observation blends with the notion of critical learning times. The importance of the early environment is perhaps the most critical of all.

Opportunity to practise

Children never fail to surprise by what they can achieve and practice does work. The two maxims together should confirm that no one should ever consider giving up supporting children even when progress is very slow. Many children with poor short-term memories need over-learning to establish routines or they need to be shown how to use feedback from one try to improve the next. This can be done through simple discussion for example: 'Your foot bumped into the bench that time. What will you do next time?' Small steps allow small achievements that can give the confidence to try again until competence is gained.

Temperament

It is thought that temperament is inherited – one of the strands of the 'genetic blueprint that influences what we can do' (Bee, 1999). Like movement competence, temperamental traits can be seen on a continuum:

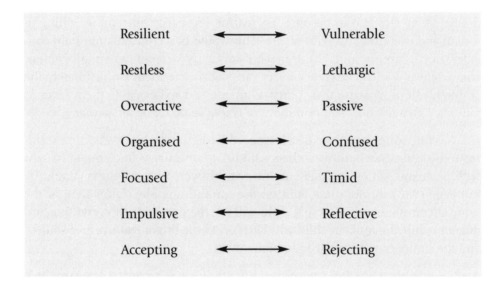

Resilient	⟷	Vulnerable
Restless	⟷	Lethargic
Overactive	⟷	Passive
Organised	⟷	Confused
Focused	⟷	Timid
Impulsive	⟷	Reflective
Accepting	⟷	Rejecting

This plethora of terms lets us understand why Thomas and Chess (1977) grouped the descriptors into three categories. These they named, 'the easy child', 'the difficult child' and 'the slow to warm up child'.

An important question, given that temperament is inherited, is, whether it is fixed, i.e. would a child described as vulnerable be so in every situation, or do the people also involved in the activity play a large part in determining the children's attitude, motivation and in turn aptitude? Is the 'difficult child' hard to control all of the time or is the child different at home and at school? Certainly studies of motivation have placed the responsibility for the child's enthusiasm in the teacher's court rather than blaming the child (Macintyre and Murdoch, 1985). This observation sees temperament as a duo or interacting phenomenon. Yet there are children brought up in the same families and with the same opportunities that are undeniably very different in the way they approach any new learning task. The impulsive ones begin a task with enthusiasm and vigour even if they lack preparation and have not thought through the consequences of what they do. They land up with finished work, often full of careless mistakes that they could have rectified had they taken more time. Reflective children, on the other hand, are ponderers who consider different strategies or alternative answers, often to the extent of not getting their work finished at all. In neither case does the product give a true indication of the children's competence. Very often in school the wrong kind of support is given. The children are given more work instead of being helped to understand why the strategy they employ is not allowing them to be successful.

Or perhaps to phrase this in a more positive mode, how can parents and teachers help children to become less fearful, less easily hurt, more willing to join in and take risks and yet stay safe? This would be a critically important consideration. Parents and children can so easily despair when movement competences, which everyone can see, are poorly executed. Unfortunately the children can often sense their parents' unease and self-evaluate themselves as failures. Often the only solution they see is to give up trying altogether.

While some from very disadvantaged backgrounds and everything seeming to be against them thrive, others with many advantages find coping fraught with problems. Of course there are no easy answers as to why this should be but Bee (1998) throws some light on the conundrum. She claims that, in the same circumstance, a vulnerable child will see the downside of everything and despair, while the resilient child will latch on to the bright features and smile – and the smiles can in turn, lead to better things.

And so any assessment – and especially any formal recorded assessment – should be made contextually, i.e. with a full picture of the background to provide explanations and reasons why. With thought and care reports home can be couched in positive terms showing the things that the children have achieved and give pointers for practice. In this way the type of report can be the same for all of the children – surely this will encourage them to keep achieving?

A new assessment tool for special needs has been devised by Wheedon and Reid. It is a computer assisted diagnostic assessment that aids profiling (for details see Bibliography).

CHAPTER 3

Learning and perception

PART 1

Learning and movement

How can one begin to understand the complex series of events called learning? This would be a huge undertaking even if children were alike in the different aspects that made up their development. But even children of the same chronological age are not the same in appearance, in temperament or in the attitudes or attributes they bring to learning. Individual children have their own set of abilities, preferences, growth patterns and environmental influences that influence what they learn and how they learn. This makes understanding each child's learning process as a means of finding ways to support them a gargantuan challenge. But of course it presents a stimulating and rewarding endeavour too and over the years researchers and learning theorists have been at pains to crack the puzzle.

Some have studied large numbers of children to discern similarities so that findings can be generalisable (i.e. apply to many children). They have tabulated their findings as norms or things 'normal' children should be able to do at specific ages. They have had to admit, however, than these timings are wide, providing only guidance to alert adults to a usual pattern of progress. The fact that the rate of progress is not smooth but at the mercy of illnesses, growth spurts, family status and culture also has to be considered in comparing any one child to some perceived norm. Other researchers have studied small numbers of children in minute detail so that they have more intimate knowledge than can be gleaned from a larger sample. The downside of this method, however, is that the findings may be specific to that small group and no claims to generalisation can be made (Macintyre, 2000). It is therefore important that those seeking to understand the process of learning should discover where the research claims are coming from. They should ask: How many children formed the sample? How long did the research continue? and How valid/enduring were the claims that were made?

As the years pass, even the 'research giants' such as Piaget are challenged. Theorists such as Donaldson and Hughes who replicated his tests (e.g. the famous three mountains test to find if children could appreciate someone else's perspective) found that using child-friendly language helped children solve the problem at an earlier age than Piaget claimed was possible; similarly with his tests of conservation that sought to find when children realised that changing the shape of something did not change its value. Children today seem to grasp the concepts needed for success at an earlier age. Perhaps this would only be surprising if children were static entities, not energetic problem-solvers as Piaget claimed. Perhaps teaching methods today are more akin to grappling with ideas rather than accumulating facts or possibly the children have a different set of experiences to guide their thinking? This is why constant revisiting and rechecking of research claims need to happen in the light of the life opportunities modern children have.

However, such findings should not detract from the wealth of knowledge that researchers have passed on, particularly as these still guide the recommended teaching strategies of today. Some particularly relevant ideas for movement learning follow.

Constructivism

Children are active participants in the development of knowledge, capable of constructing their own understanding. In so doing they learn to adapt to the world. Most developmental theorists accept this proposition known as constructivism. (Flavell, 1992)

This idea underlies the ethos of child-centred learning based on adults observing what the children do and intervening only when they know how to extend learning appropriately. Practioners have become resource managers. They require the skill to observe and understand what resources are needed to extend the children's learning in the most appropriate way. This is a huge shift in emphasis from filling the children with facts that they 'ought to know' and engaging them in activities they 'ought to have'. And as they do this they have the very difficult task of building interactions to extend the children's language while engaging them in meaningful conversations. They have to be able to promote thinking through asking open-ended questions or sharing experiences. This is much more challenging than asking closed questions which tends to cut down the children's contributions.

Unfortunately (in my view), in some early years nurseries and more often in classrooms, the pressure of meeting targets has meant that more formal learning has to be imposed on the children. Perhaps in the desire to be 'top', educators have not considered the wider social, emotional and timely learning needs of very young children? Perhaps they mistrust Piaget's (1972) claim that children have the competence and capacity to be scientists? Or perhaps they have not heeded Cohen's (1996) question, 'Are there social engineers on the swings?'

The active learner has to be one that moves to explore the environment, hence Piaget's claim that 'The child's first language is movement', i.e. planning, organising, doing. What sorts of abilities are being developed?

- Making choices, e.g. what to do

- Selecting resources to fulfil a task

- Lifting, manipulating, placing, pouring

- Matching, sorting, tracking, moulding

- Walking, running, climbing, sliding, etc

- Sequencing, i.e. deciding what needs to be done first, then next

- Following instructions about safety

- Sharing, co-operating, working alongside, discussing, planning in twos

- Balancing, making spacial decisions, working rhythmically, using the appropriate amount of strength and speed

- Throwing and catching, kicking, etc.

All of these provide an opportunity for observation and assessment. As the children carry out these experiments, movement difficulties can be in evidence before any others, e.g. social or intellectual, are displayed. Careful observation can ensure that remedial measures are immediately put in place.

The pace of new learning

The pace of new learning has to be carefully considered to ensure equilibrium. Again this is a Piagetian construct. He explained that too much new material would confuse children while too much repetition would bore them. He asked teachers to have a balanced approach in their selection of material. This sounds like common sense so why is it worth repeating? There are two reasons why. Firstly, even very young children complain of being bored at school, and if they are, the balance is not working. Could it be that they do not have enough freedom to move and to explore? Secondly, it is very difficult for teachers to select material that will fulfil the needs of each of thirty children who all require different competences to be nurtured. Arranging classes in chronological age groups really doesn't address the issue at all.

Matching teaching and learning styles

Children learn in different ways. Teachers should recognise and adapt their own teaching style to achieve a match and thus facilitate the children's learning.

The ideal, i.e. that parents and teachers should self-evaluate their own teaching method, is not new. The critical question is: 'How realistic is it for teachers to make the shift and adopt the children's way?' Certainly providing balance in the curriculum so that competences such as imagination and creative work are given their fair share is one step but how readily can a convergent thinker become divergent in the real sense of providing appropriate stimulation, resources and encouragement to children who learn in a very different way from their own? In the busyness of the classroom possibly not everyone would be able to make that shift. Nonetheless it is an ideal to strive for!

Certainly the features of specific learning difficulties have to be understood by all practioners so that appropriate reinforcement and learning accommodations can be given. One of the most successful recent interventions is the daily movement programme that has been shown to give confidence alongside competence. Another move is to provide laptops for children who find writing very difficult. This allows the children to keep up with their peers and function according to their level of intelligence. Not all schools are willing to do this but the relief felt by many children would seem to me to outweigh notions of 'having to be able to write well'.

Offering support

Vygotsky's (1978) 'zone of proximal development' advising parents and practioners to gauge the children's immediate potential and to support them so that 'tomorrow they will be able to do alone the task they had help with today' is a popular tenet (similar to Bruner's (1966) idea of scaffolding). Perhaps less well known is the idea of dynamic assessment which sprang from that idea.

Dynamic assessment endeavours to assess the process of learning rather than measuring attainment according to some standardised test. This involves observing how the children tackle tasks and the problem-solving (metacognitive) strategies they use. The reaction of children to carefully structured assistance and the response to success or failure is noted as well as the memory/functional approaches. It is hoped that this will provide insights into the children's processing difficulties and so alert practioners to the most appropriate ways to offer support (www.dynamicassessment.com). Such moves show the current endeavours to understand what is happening as children learn.

Physically supporting children as they move

In the past, practioners literally 'gave a hand' to children to help them balance along a bench or tackle other challenges for the first time. This was a temporary measure till the children gained confidence to do the activity themselves. Today of course practioners are advised not to touch children at all. In many establishments, the result has been to reduce the movement challenges to 'what the children can do alone'. The most agile children are therefore denied challenge. And yet offering support was what Vygotsky advised. The practioners were 'gauging what the child would be able to do tomorrow' and intervening appropriately; the difference was the support was visualised as being in the intellectual not the physical domain. Perhaps the idea of 'touching children' needs to be rethought and parameters set out so that there can be a little leeway to allow some support while still keeping the children free from interference.

Critical learning periods

Researchers into 'critical learning periods' are divided in their beliefs as to whether skill can be recaptured if the experience is missing at key learning times or whether other factors prevent the acquisition of the skill. Think of an adult learning to ski as the 4-year-old whizzes past. The adult would still be able to learn but it could take longer, provided of course that the temperament to persevere was not shaken by the image of the skilled child. Another negative vibe could come from the humiliation or the actual hurt of falling! In that case temperament in the form of resilience would play a big part!

In all research outside the laboratory it is very difficult to determine causation, i.e. that one thing definitely caused another thing to change. This is especially difficult in research with children because of other variables which could influence them. Hence the debates and discussions which throw up conflicting theories within education. For example, there is much debate as to the existence and importance of critical times in learning diffrerent skills.

But perhaps the least well researched area is perception or how children take in cues to help them understand and respond to the environment around them. Part 2 of this chapter considers these issues.

Perception

All learning takes place in the brain but it is the body which acts as the vehicle by which knowledge is acquired. Both brain and body work together through the central nervous system but both are dependent on the senses for all information about the outside world. (Goddard, 2002)

To be equipped to learn three basic sensory systems have to function well, namely

■ the reception of information through the senses (*perception*);

■ the processing of information in the brain (*analysis*);

■ the response by the efferent system (*outcome*).

This part of the chapter considers the way in which children's sensory input affects their movement and their learning. It is very important to understand this, because from the moment of birth children are bombarded by sensory information and they are required to perceive and analyse it all in order to make sense of what is happening around them. What, then, are the different senses?

There are eight, yet when children learn about the senses at home and at school, they usually only hear about five – hearing, seeing, touching, tasting and smelling. Rarely, if ever, do they mention the sixth, the sense of balance, yet this one, which depends on the vestibular sense, may be the most important one of all for it is a fundamental requisite of all the activities of daily living. Then there are the kinaesthetic and proprioceptive senses, perhaps even less well known yet they provide critical information about the position of the body in space. If all of the senses are functioning well, their contribution is hardly noticed yet if one or other is 'faulty' then they affect the children's participation in everything they do.

Also important is the fact that from the earliest days, none of these senses work in isolation – they all combine their effects to impact on movement and learning. This process is known as sensory integration (Ayres, 1972) or cross modal transfer (Bee, 2001).This collusion or integration may have a positive or negative effect on the outcome depending on how much one aspect of perception can boost or suppress the other. Certainly the overlap makes analysis and assessment of individual sensory contributions difficult. Poor sight may make children stumble and fall just as poor spatial awareness (kinaesthesis) can, yet children tend to have their individual senses tested by different specialists. Each expert then treats or 'corrects' the specific deficit, possibly without considering any other source of sensory input. As a result, when one sense is 'changed', the children are left having to adapt to a different set of impulses.

A critically important point is that when sensory demands increase (i.e. when the children have to carry out more complex tasks or become more independent), if one sense is not functioning properly, then primitive reflexes that have been inhibited by maturation may come into play again. If the Moro reflex was re-alerted as just one example, the child would see the world as too bright and too loud – as a booming, buzzing confusion. This would result in the child being tense and stressed, constantly ready to 'flee' and possibly at the mercy of allergies and irritations (Goddard, 2002).

On the other hand, the asymmetric tonic neck reflex could be invoked. This means that when the head is turned to one side, the reflex causes the arm on the same side to stretch out. It is therefore difficult to control a pencil to write and draw without strain because the hand has to be pulled back into the writing position. Reading could be affected too because of difficulties in tracking the print, especially when the eyes have to cross the midline. These difficulties would cause hesitation and lack of fluency so that the meaning of the text could be lost, this despite comprehension per se not being a problem. In such subtleties lie the misdiagnoses which occur when time or expertise/precision in observation is lacking.

An example might help to clarify the sensory integration that happens all of the time as children learn.

Example 4

Learning to ride a bike

Most children want to learn to ride a bike. What contribution do the senses make? How do they work together to help the necessary skills be acquired?

▶

The most obvious new skill that the children must learn is to balance on a narrow base when they are off the ground in a new unstable environment. The vestibular sense makes a key contribution here. As they do this, they have to look ahead (visual sense) to see where to go and decide which path looks manageable. If their spatial awareness (the kinaesthetic sense) is functioning well they will be able to judge distance and so appreciate how far they should travel and the direction in which they should go. This implicitly gives them information about how hard they need to push each pedal and which part of the foot to use to apply the correct amount of strength (the tactile sense). The auditory sense lets them judge the distance from obstacles or other cyclists and so keeps them safe. The sense of smell can have a similar function if ditches are nearby! No mention yet of the proprioceptive sense, but it makes a very important contribution to success. The proprioceptors in the nerves and skin relay positional information and so let the children feel where their body parts are without looking to see, i.e. without using the visual sense. It is not difficult to recognise the effect on balance if the children had to bend over to check whether their feet were firmly on the pedals! If they had to do this, they would be using their visual sense to compensate for their poor proprioceptive one.

The senses will now be given their 'real' names (see Figure 3.1) and will be considered in turn.

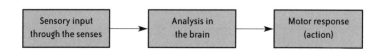

Figure 3.1 Sensory perception.

The vestibular sense

The vestibular sense is the first of the senses to develop functioning even before birth to give the foetus a sense of direction within the womb, a sense which develops to help the child cope with gravity from the moment of birth. And of course this competence is essential if children are to be in control of their bodies as they meet different balance challenges as they grow. The baby who has to realign after being turned over in the cot and the toddler who learns to crawl round obstacles is practising the skills needed to become the dancer who can spin with control or the footballer who swerves and dodges while controlling a ball!

If there are difficulties in the vestibular system then there are implications for all the other senses. This is because all the input from the other senses passes through the vestibular at the level of the brainstem. This being so, 'what we see, hear and feel only makes sense if the vestibular is functioning properly' (Pyper, and Johnston, 1981).

The vestibular sense is located in the inner ear. It has two main parts consisting of three semicircular canals and two vestibular sacs, all lined by hairs and filled with fluid. This combination reacts to the movements of the head by releasing impulses along the 8th cranial nerve pathway. If there is too much sway, motion sickness results and it becomes very difficult to maintain an upright stance. This is extremely unpleasant. Some children and adults, however, actually seek out experiences such as fairground rides or bungie jumping. They are just in control but their sense of balance is tested to the full. This kind of activity is known as the pursuit of vertigo. More usually, upsets in the normal level of fluid activity within the ear are very distressing. This can happen with illnesses such as labyrinthitis when nausea and dizziness accompany feelings of being off balance.

Vestibular input is vital in both movement (dynamic balance) and stillness (static balance). Difficulties suggesting a poor vestibular sense include:

- constant movement;
- falling over – evidence of a poor sense of balance;
- dislike of movements that require them to leave the ground;
- delay in acquiring motor milestones, e.g. slow to gain control of the head and body in sitting unsupported as well as in walking;
- poor sense of direction leading to poor organisational and planning skills;
- tiredness due to constant concentration when spatial decision-making is not automatic.

These could all be indicators of specific learning difficulties, e.g. dyspraxia, dyslexia, Asperger's syndrome, as well as being part of global developmental delay or neurological problems.

The auditory sense

This sense shares the location with the vestibular one – the cochlea or auditory apparatus shares a chamber, fluid and transmission along the same cranial nerve. The auditory sense allows judgement of direction, e.g. how far away something is, and timing, e.g. when and how fast to move. The ear transmits vibrations to the brain which are relayed as sound.

Young children can have recurring ear infections and other hearing impairments such as glue ear that can hamper the development of both listening skills and early language. It is critically important that sounds should be heard clearly at the correct developmental time. It is understandably difficult for children to sustain paying attention if sounds are blurred. Difficulty in distinguishing separate sounds, especially those that have similar sounds, can lead to difficulty with spelling and reading.

Auditory distractibility

Although some children can hear clearly, they can be distracted by the least sound in the environment around them. They seem unable to ignore these sounds and so their concentration is disturbed. If they are hypersensitive to sound then even a low level of noise can disturb them to the point that they must find a way to remove themselves from its source. They either withdraw or rebel, often to the dismay of parents, teachers and friends. Neither strategy is a winning solution.

When adults claim that children don't listen, perhaps this is because they have been rendered unable to listen by the bustle around them. Their learning environment has to be constructed so that they are enabled to hear. If difficulties persist, investigations with an audiologist have to be carried out without delay.

Many children prefer to have a workstation apart from the other children so that the buzz of the classroom is reduced. Adults have to understand that even the rustle of paper can be distressing or at least diverting so that work becomes delayed. Yet no one would want the children to feel isolated so careful selection of a quiet spot is more difficult that it would seem. Parents can help by vacuuming or doing DIY when the hypersensitive child is out of range and by remembering that the constant noise of the television can be upsetting. Wooden floors are not helpful as the noise of heels reverberates!

The effects of 'no sound'

The corollary of too much sound is the effect of being deprived of all sound and so having no auditory cues to tell what is going on in the environment. Sounds can be comforting, assuring the listeners that they are safe. Sound deprivation can become as unbearable as continuous, strident sound.

Difficulties suggesting a poor auditory sense include:

■ inattention;

■ inability to follow sequential instructions;

■ mistakes in spelling and reading due to confused sounds;

■ delay in responding (possibly compensating by using another sense);

■ hypersensitivity to sounds;

■ singing out of tune and with poor awareness of rhythm;

■ being easily distracted by the slightest sound.

The tactile sense

Touch receptors cover the entire body allowing children to react appropriately to different levels of pressure. While most children enjoy a hug and actively seek out close contact, others have a different reaction. They are hypersensitive, i.e. feeling the touch too fiercely. Even a gentle pat can cause discomfort. Alternatively some children need pressure to feel secure. They need to be tucked in tightly at night and some prefer weighty bedclothes to a light cover, even in summer! Yet again some children are hyposensitive, i.e. lacking awareness of their own strength. An example of this would be the child who constantly breaks toys or the leads in crayons because of excess pressure. When things just come apart in one's hands, when 'Mr Nobody' is to blame, tactile hyposensitivity may be the cause.

The area in the brain which deals with touch is the somatosensory cortex. It registers pain, heat, cold and pressure as well as body position. The different pain thresholds that children feel are down to this sense. Children who are sensitive to pain can be very distressed by having their hair or nails cut because touch receptors are in each hair follicle and in the nail beds. Adults who don't understand may wonder why the child is making so much fuss. It is vitally important that adults also recognise that some children do not feel internal pain and may become ill with no complaint. This can cause parents a great deal of worry.

The link with spatial awareness (the kinaesthetic sense) can be seen when some children with overdeveloped tactile sensitivity cannot bear anyone to intrude into their personal space. They may well panic when this happens and hit out. This incident may well be 'dealt with' without seeking out the underlying cause. 'Lining up' can be really difficult for these children so having them as 'back of the line monitor' removes the stress without making them feel different or inadequate.

Difficulties suggesting a poor tactile sense include:

- heightened sensitivity or lack of tactile awareness;

- reluctance to be in close contact with others;

- hitting out to protect personal space;

- avoidance of being touched;

- too willing to touch others.

The visual sense

The most obvious visual disability comes when children are short sighted or have an astigmatism and need specialist input to help them see more clearly. Without this, the impact on many aspects of academic learning that depend on the visual sense must be significant. The picture seen by each eye must be clear and they must function together to give a focused image. If not, children may see overlapping or blurred shapes; they may see two 'O's on the page when there is only one or see the notes on musical notation conceverge or diverge when attempting to play a tune. It is not difficult to imagine how this affects reading skills. Some children are light sensitive and find reflections and strong lights cause real discomfort; indeed the words on the classroom white-board may be totally obscured. These difficulties can exacerbate a tracking problem that causes children to lose their place as they read or copy items from one place to the next.

But the visual sense has a much wider remit. It is critically important in helping the body to move in a balanced controlled way. Even the most prac-tised ballet dancers have to learn to fix their eyes on a steady spot 'out there' to help them control their spins and finish facing the right direction! The visual sense also helps to compensate for poor body awareness, although over-dependence on the visual causes a delay in responding. A good test is to ask children to walk in a straight line forwards heel to toe. Those who have to look down to check the position of their feet may well lose their balance.

Difficulties suggesting a poor visual sense include:

■ rubbing the eyes, peering, holding the text very close to the face;

■ a delay in responding to tasks;

■ losing the place while reading or copying;

■ holding the hands up to reduce glare;

■ putting objects down with a clatter (due to misjudging the space);

■ being tired and frustrated through struggling to focus.

The senses of taste and smell

These senses are well known as they function to stimulate appetites or warn that food is no longer fresh. But tastes and smells can evoke memories of happy times – perhaps a woodland fire can recall days when scouts or guides sang round the bonfire while disinfectant can conjure up images of painful times spent in hospital or even school toilets. Strong smells, e.g. tar on the road, can also help tell how far away things are and so help directionality. And of course being able to smell food stimulates the production of saliva which helps the sense of taste. The two senses work together, not in isolation.

Normally, unpleasant tastes and smells can be shrugged off as a temporary inconvenience but some children are hypersensitive, especially to strong smelling aerosols or even expensive perfumes. The level that reaches all of us is not the same. On the other hand many children relish spicy curries and highly flavoured crisps. Some children will even attempt to eat pills and potions which have been specially designed to be unpalatable as a safety mechanism.

Difficulties suggesting a poor sense of taste and/or smell include:

■ avoiding places and people because they 'smell';

■ poor appetite because of intolerance of food smells;

■ willingness to eat/drink unsuitable items or fluids;

■ intolerance of smells other people find pleasant.

The proprioceptive sense

The proprioceptors are nerve endings in the muscles, joints, tendons and skin. They relay positional information to tell children where there body parts are in relation to one another. Being able to feel where the chair supports their thighs, for example, or where the fingers have to go to grip a pencil allows movements to be precise and co-ordinated. When the proprioceptive sense is functioning well, the children have a clear idea of their posture and they can make adjustments. If they are asked to 'shrug your shoulders and let them drop', for example when the teacher is trying to get them to relax (raised shoulders are often a sign of tension and feeling the difference between shrugging and relaxing is a useful teaching strategy), the children should be able to do this without having to look to see where these parts are. When that happens, the visual sense is being asked to compensate for a poor proprioceptive one.

The input is processed through the vestibular sense and works with all other sensory sources to aid balance and efficient movement, i.e. with no fluster or clumsiness. It is a complex sense because incorrect information coming from any of the other senses will affect the proprioceptive sense. It can also work to give a sense of position when the visual and auditory senses are not functioning well. This means that deaf/blind children can still orientate themselves in space and can adjust their bodies, e.g. to find a better balanced position.

Even at rest (and this is where the proprioceptive sense differs from the kinaesthetic), the proprioceptive sense should be providing positional information that helps keep the body balanced and secure. Poor proprioception is common in children with learning difficulties (Goddard, 2002). Children who move too much may have a poorly functioning proprioceptive sense. They are trying to stimulate their proprioceptors to give them information about the position of their body in space. Times of rest are hard to handle because of this lack of input.

The kinaesthetic sense

Sometimes the names proprioceptive and kinaesthetic are used interchangeably, but strictly speaking they are not the same. The kinaesthetic sense comes into play when the body is in action and so is instrumental in giving spatial and directional advice. Judgements such as 'how far away is the wall or the kerb?' depend on spatial orientation.

A poor kinaesthetic sense can result in children running into objects that are in their path, or dropping things because they have not 'measured' the space between their hand and the table accurately. Children can often be accused of barging and bumping because they have not been able to judge whether their bodies will fit through a space or not!

In a position of rest, the proprioceptors work alone but once movement begins, the kinaesthetic sense complements the other. As they work together, the symptoms of poor input are given as one group.

Difficulties suggesting poor proprioceptive and kinesthetic input

These include:

- a general clumsiness – fumbling rather than precise movement;

- an inability to be still for a reasonable amount of time;

- looking at feet or hands to check where they are;

- a slight hesitation in reacting to instructions;

- avoidance of sedentary activities;

- using too much pressure, e.g. when using a pencil or playing the piano;

- using an inappropriate amount of strength to kick a ball.

The regulation of all the sensory input is important if children are to cope without stress in a complex ever-changing and often chemical-laden environment. The kind of sensation that is received will affect the response that is given. All the senses should work together in harmony and then movement and learning can happen almost without conscious planning although, in truth, many sophisticated processes are taking place. The more evident sensory difficulties such as poor vision or hearing may be easier to spot than tactile or proprioceptive problems, but whichever are apparent intervention needs to take place so that the impact on learning is reduced.

Some questions for parents to consider

Obviously parents know their children best and they have the opportunity to observe them in many different situations. This should make them ideal observers; however, over time many aspects of the children's behaviour (the ways they do things, not whether they are good or badly behaved) become taken for granted or become lost in the busyness of the day. Some prompts about how the children react at home can help pinpoint areas where sensory support might be required.

The vestibular sense

- Does your child move constantly, i.e. seem unable to settle?

- Is your child a poor sleeper, always ready for more activity?

- Does your child avoid swings or chutes, etc., i.e. seem fearful of a moving base?

- Is your child tentative in climbing stairs, perhaps using a feet together pattern rather than a single foot on each step?

- Does your child get carsick?

- Does your child 'fall over thin air'?

- Does your child take a 'bull in a china shop' approach, i.e. getting there, no matter who is in the way?

The auditory sense

- Does your child often appear to be in a world of his own, i.e. cutting out other noises?

- Does your child hear sounds that are missed by others?

- Does your child become upset by noise, e.g. the vacuum cleaner, or washing machine or a sibling's music?

- Does your child hide away 'to get a bit of peace and quiet' when the noise level for others is low?

- Does your child make lots of noise and seem relaxed while others are upset by the clamour?

- Does your child shout out inappropriately?

The tactile sense

- Is your child irritated by seams in clothes or socks?

- Does your child resist hugs and cuddles?

- Does your child avoid being touched yet seem anxious to touch others?

- Does washing hair or face and/or cutting nails cause real distress?

- Does your child-appear oblivious of pain or overreact to minor scratches and bumps?

- Is your child over protective of personal space and does 'intrusion' cause over-reaction?

- Does your child show no reaction to being touched?

- Does your child constantly fiddle with hair or pieces of cloth, etc.?

- Does your child have a 'normal' reaction to pain?

The visual sense

- Does your child 'peer' or hold books, etc. very close to the face?

- Does strong light worry the child?

- Does your child explain that letters move on the page?

- Can your child only focus briefly then have to look away?

- Is your child annoyed/distressed/overly distracted by visual stimuli and so lose concentration?

- Does your child find justified print difficult?

- Does coloured paper make a difference?

- Does your child have difficulty seeing objects as distinct from their background?

- Does your child have difficulty tracking, e.g. following the path of a ball, the words on a page or copying shapes or drawings?

The proprioceptive sense

- Does your child seem 'all over the place', i.e. unaware where arms and legs are?

- Does your child not use enough pressure, e.g. have wispy thin writing and drawing?

- Does your child seek out pressure, e.g. thump feet down hard to get a sense of position?

- Does your child want to be tucked in well at bedtime?

- Is your child reassured by being hugged?

- Does your child have a clear picture of the position of different body parts and the relation of one to the other?

The kinaesthetic sense

- Is your child forever bumping into things?

- Does your child have a poor sense of direction?

- Does your child get lost in what should be familiar territory?

- Is your child reluctant to visit new places, especially if unaccompanied?

- Does your child understand maps?

- Can your child go for a message and come back?

The senses of taste and smell

- Is your child willing to try new tastes?

- Will your child tolerate only a limited diet?

- Does your child eat strange 'non-food items', e.g. coal, dog biscuits?

- Is your child distressed by strong smells, e.g. disinfectant in kitchens and toilets?

- Can your child tolerate ordinary smells/smells which are pleasant to others?

It can be seen from the lists above that both hyper (over) and hypo (under) reactions to sensory information cause children to behave differently. They do not understand why and 'trying harder' is not a real solution. A carefully planned programme of activities that stress sensory integration can do much to relieve immediate difficulties and also help future learning, for 'the brain that cannot organise sensory input cannot organise letters and numbers' (Ayres, 1972).

CHAPTER 4

Handwriting and mathematics –
a movement perspective

Handwriting

Note. There are many texts on 'how to teach writing'. This one stresses the movement aspect of the skill. It stresses that pre-writing movement activities can significantly boost the underlying competences that are based on motor control and sensory integration. Many children have to begin formal writing 'too soon', i.e. according to their chronological age rather than their developmental stage. How, then, can these children have the motor control to write?

Handwriting is a very important motor skill. There are six attainment targets for children between 5 and 11 years and failing to meet these can restrict opportunities for progress right across the curriculum. It is important that children are taught to produce legible writing and this involves teachers recognising the sensory–motor competences that underlie the skill. The input of sensory information from the environment requires analysis and translation in the brain, which in turn must convey the correct instructions to the muscles, especially those in the shoulders, arms, wrists and fingers. Being a good writer also depends on having the necessary balance, hand–eye co-ordination, appropriate physical strength, hand awareness and a clear sense of direction as well as the correct resources, yet many who aim to teach are unsure of assessing these underlying competences. Recognising them all is necessary to discern the children's readiness to accomplish what is, after all, a complex undertaking. In addition, and possibly as a result of this, children are often asked to write, i.e. to visualise the letter forms and to scribe them, before they have enough pre-writing activities such as drawing circles, shapes and straight lines on large pieces of paper. These pre-writing activities are essential in developing hand dominance and hand–eye co-ordination. Without them it is no wonder that some children fail.

Games such as join the dots or mazes are invaluable in developing pencil control and a sense of direction (the lines of the walls of the maze can be adjusted to match the children's competence). Essentially, all of these are pre-writing practices. Other activities that can make a significant input are working with plasticene and clay, for these encourage hand strength and hand awareness as the children watch their fingers as they mould. Playing the piano helps children to concentrate on their fingers and move each one in isolation from the rest quite apart from them enjoying the musical feedback. Popping bubble paper gives irresistible feedback too and the action can help dexterity through strengthening the fingers. There are many activities that develop the very necessary movement skills. They give variety as well as practice and so prevent the children from insisting that they 'can't write' – a self evaluation which can be hard to shift.

Samantha is strengthening her fingers by moulding and pressing. The cutting action helps working at the midline of the body.

Parents are often concerned that inputs like those mentioned above are 'only play', that they are taking up teaching time and that their children should be 'doing real writing'. This can pressurise teachers into starting formal writing too soon. They are afraid the parents will complain and/or decide to intervene and instruct the children themselves. This strategy often results in the children having to unlearn the names and sounds of letters as well as how they are formed. This can cause resentment all round! But why is there this pressure?

Most people would regard handwriting as a key learning tool. It is used extensively throughout school to communicate thoughts and ideas and record calculations. 'Good handwriting' leads to 'neat work', often a source of praise, especially in the early years. In fact the immediate impact of poor handwriting (see Figure 4.1) can disguise the content of what is written to the extent that assessments are distorted by focusing on poor letter formation and word layout rather than the imaginative content or even the structure of the story or the poem. And of course, handwriting involves writing numbers too. Poor number formation may even cause a sum to be marked wrong when the answer is correct.

CASE STUDY

Alex aged 8, is upset after being asked to write out her homework again:
'She says I've to do it again and I can't. My hands are too tired and my eyes aren't wanting to do it anyway. My head knows what to do, but even when I go slowly my writing comes out all wrong. I never get my story put up on the wall. I've to read mine out to the class and they all clap and that makes me feel really good but when Mum comes to see how I'm getting on she's told I'm still a messy writer. She says to try harder but it doesn't work. One day I got my sums wrong and I had exactly the same answers as Sam and he got no crosses. Anyway he was copying me so I know we had the same. I don't know why I'm worst in the whole class, but I am.'

Parents and teachers expect children to be able to write well so there is often an implicit pressure on children to achieve a legible, even an attractive script. It is not difficult to imagine the negative effect on the children's self-esteem when they are constantly chided for untidy or illegible work. Very often they can be told to 'do it again.' This may sound reasonable until one recognises that, for many children, repetition only results in resentment, distress and possibly exhaustion with a second effort no better than the first.

The trouble is that sometimes adults who try to help don't know why either. Being able to produce legible handwriting is often taken for granted and the 'remedy' suggested is 'do it more carefully'. The effort that poor writers have to put in to make even a short piece of work legible is incredible, yet some writing schemes ask children to make a rough copy, discuss improvements with the teacher, then copy the same passage out neatly. Although the finished article may be enhanced (for those who are not turned off by the boredom of repetition), the demand on handwriting has been doubled causing anguish to those who find this aspect of the task so difficult.

So what is involved in being able to write and how can children who find writing difficult be helped? Handwriting is a complex movement skill. It is a 'visible trace of the movement of the hand' (Sassoon, 1998). What competences are involved?

The children need:

- a sense of hand preference/dominance, i.e. developed laterality;

- to be able to recognise/visualise/remember the pattern of the letter or word that is to be scribed;

- the strength and control in their shoulder, arm and hand to follow the pattern that is visualised or has to be copied;

- the necessary movement abilities, e.g. being able to be still, to cross the midline of the body, to have the hand–eye co-ordination to cope;

- enough spactial/kinaesthetic competence to enable them to judge the size, shape and order of the letters/numbers and the space required between different lines;

- the correct resources – table, chair, pencil, paper;

- enough space on the desktop so that the writing hand and arm is not restricted and allows the correct postioning of the paper.

These requirements are considered in further detail below.

A sense of hand preference/dominance

If children do not have a strong sense of which hand or foot they prefer to use they are likely to be confused by ambiguity of laterality (Goddard, 2002). This results in their being unsure how to pick up a pencil or kick a ball. Sometimes observing the children to note their preference then reminding them to use that hand or foot can be enough. A simple test, e.g. placing a toy on a table equidistant from each hand and then asking the child to reach to grasp it, can show whether a sense of hand dominance (repeatedly using the same hand) or confusion (not recognising that one hand gives better results) is present. This should be repeated several times using different sizes and shapes of objects, e.g. a bead, a pine cone and a larger ball. The variations in weight and size require different amounts of strength and so present different levels of challenge.

Hand choice does not always become automatic and if this doesn't happen, the children have to make a conscious decision instead of an imme-diate, 'unthinking' response. Inevitably this causes delay and possibly fumbling when changes from one hand to the other are made. There is also the possibility of retained primitive reflexes hindering progress. Goddard explains that a retained asymmetrical tonic neck reflex will prevent the chil-dren crossing the midline of the body and so manipulating a pencil, unscrewing a lid or passing something from hand to hand as opposed to using one hand only will be problematic. She has a specific series of exercises to counteract the effect of retained primitive reflexes like this. (This is 'The developmental exercise programme' – for information, contact the Institute for Neurophysiological Psychology (INPP), 4 Stanley Place, Chester CH1 2LU (tel. 01244 311414).)

Ability to recognise/visualise/remember the pattern of the letter or word

The first observation should concern reflection, asking whether the children remember what they learned yesterday. Generally, this can be discovered quite readily by asking the children to recap. If remembering is a problem – and many children, especially those with specific learning difficulties, have poor short-term memories – then over-learning using different strategies as prompts or reinforcers as well as repetition is the way forward. These could also take the form of advance organisers (Ausubel, 1963), e.g. plastic letters or numbers set out on a table or a short video clip of letters and numbers. These act as helpful reminders of what was learned yesterday.

Using different senses to help memorising

If the children have games where they can feel the letters (e.g. feely bags) this helps them internalise their shape. Then visualisation and recall is eased. When they do feel the corners and curves, their kinaesthetic sense is being used to help their visual one. In addition, saying the letters out loud can help recognition of the shape. Perhaps jingles could help too, for example see opposite.

Helping children appreciate the rhythm in words, phrases and rhymes can help both reading and writing – the latter because saying the sound as part of a rhythm helps the flow of the pattern. There have been claims by researchers at the University of London that a poor sense of rhythm could be a key difficulty in dyslexia. This is because those affected are unable to detect the beats in each word. Advanced readers on the other hand are better then average at spotting the sound effect. The earliest rhythmic learning comes through hearing the beats in the conversation. Could this be why parents instinctively emphasise/change the pattern of 'normal' speech when they coo to babies or why Mums use 'motherese'?

Many different ways of recognising and establishing shapes can be provided through movement learning activities for example:

- finding all the 'o' shapes in a basket of musical percussion (tambour, tambourine, Indian bells, cymbals, round the body of maracas, etc.);

n with persistent difficulties should be referred for speech and lan-
herapy.

arents and practioners should also, as a matter of course, check
r the children are hearing the sounds clearly by asking them to repeat a
red sound. If the children have difficulty distinguishing between
s they should be referred to an audiologist to have their hearing
d. Otherwise they will be confused and learning to read and spell will
blematic too.

strength and control in their shoulder,
and hand

f the earliest assessments children have is whether they are beginning to
e pincer grip rather than a whole-hand grasp. This is developed in nurs-
hools through activities such as threading beads or picking up small
s of material or paper at the gluing tray. A well-defined pincer grip helps
cquisition of the correct tripod pencil grip and actions such as writing to
ecise. It depends on strength in the shoulders, arms and fingers, hand
eness and dexterity.

i is learning to 'let go'. He is paying close attention and judging when to
ease the strength in his fingers. This will help develop the pincer and
pod grips and so help writing, drawing, and other fine motor skill. He is
o learning about balance.

- identifying plastic letter shapes within

- drawing letters in the sand or on the ba
  who has to identify them;

- making letter shapes with plasticine – o
  make name brooches or ornaments witl

- sorting shapes into jagged and round on
  similarities/differences, e.g. closing up th
  the 'u' turned upside down is like 'n'.

The children also need to link the shape with the
encouraged to say the sound as they feel the sl

Childr
guage t

wheth
whisp
sound
checke
be pro

The
arm

One
use tl
ery s
piece
the a
be p
awai

'O' goes round and round and round
Listen, it makes an eerie sound
Say it quietly, whisper low
Then shout it out loud,
O! O! O!

'g's a sound t
Look at its tai
Before you dra
To make the to

's' is just a slithery snake
Look at the pattern it can make
Start at the top and curl halfway,
Then go back the other way

'l' is a long thin
'Standing very ta
Make your arms
Be careful not to

Children with verbal dyspraxia also need practise in makii
is difficult, exercises to develop the strength in the muscle
be helpful. These might include:

- blowing bubbles;

- sucking through a straw;

- chewing thickly cut bread and jam.

Ka
re
tri
al

8

■ identifying plastic letter shapes within a feely bag;

■ drawing letters in the sand or on the back of another child who has to identify them;

■ making letter shapes with plasticine – older children can make name brooches or ornaments with clay;

■ sorting shapes into jagged and round ones and discussing the similarities/differences, e.g. closing up the 'c' letter gives 'o', the 'u' turned upside down is like 'n'.

The children also need to link the shape with the sound so they have to be encouraged to say the sound as they feel the shape or trace the pattern.

'O' goes round and round and round
Listen, it makes an eerie sound
Say it quietly, whisper low
Then shout it out loud,
O! O! O!

'g's a sound thats starts off gown
Look at its tail, it's hanging down
Before you draw the tail, be sure
To make the top part quite secure.

's' is just a slithery snake
Look at the pattern it can make
Start at the top and curl halfway,
Then go back the other way

'l' is a long thin letter
'Standing very tall
Make your arms stretch up like that
Be careful not to fall!

Children with verbal dyspraxia also need practise in making the sounds. If this is difficult, exercises to develop the strength in the muscles in the mouth can be helpful. These might include:

■ blowing bubbles;

■ sucking through a straw;

■ chewing thickly cut bread and jam.

Children with persistent difficulties should be referred for speech and language therapy.

Parents and practioners should also, as a matter of course, check whether the children are hearing the sounds clearly by asking them to repeat a whispered sound. If the children have difficulty distinguishing between sounds they should be referred to an audiologist to have their hearing checked. Otherwise they will be confused and learning to read and spell will be problematic too.

The strength and control in their shoulder, arm and hand

One of the earliest assessments children have is whether they are beginning to use the pincer grip rather than a whole-hand grasp. This is developed in nursery schools through activities such as threading beads or picking up small pieces of material or paper at the gluing tray. A well-defined pincer grip helps the acquisition of the correct tripod pencil grip and actions such as writing to be precise. It depends on strength in the shoulders, arms and fingers, hand awareness and dexterity.

Kai is learning to 'let go'. He is paying close attention and judging when to release the strength in his fingers. This will help develop the pincer and tripod grips and so help writing, drawing, and other fine motor skill. He is also learning about balance.

Pencil grip

Children must have a grip that is comfortable for them else their hand will soon become tired, their shoulders tense and their writing will show the strain. Although there is a recognised tripod grip that many children adopt quite naturally, other children choose another grip and assert that they can manage very well. Often this claim is belied when they are required to write at speed or for a length of time. So it is a good idea to have children draw flowing patterns before they tackle letters (see Figure 4.1). Teachers can then observe how the chosen grip will affect the flow or the accuracy of the pattern. The question of whether children should be 'made to use the correct grip' has been the source of many discussions. Even experts disagree! Kiely (1996) suggests that 'if an unorthodox grip gives no problems, then there is no need to try to change it'. However, Hornsby (1984) disagrees. She explains that 'it should also be remembered that "unlearning" an awkward grip is difficult, so perhaps it is best to encourage the correct grip from the start'. Perhaps this depends on whether the children can be persuaded to change or indeed whether they are able to do so. (See also the comments on left-handed children later in the chapter). Certainly practising drawing large flowing patterns can let the children experience different ways of holding and controlling a pencil or a brush as they 'use their own written marks to express their feelings and thoughts' (SCCC, 1999).

Trying out different pencil grips

If the children experience difficulty in establishing a grip that allows them to be successful, it is a good idea to try out the variety of commercially produced pencil grips which provide a thicker stem. Very often these help small fingers

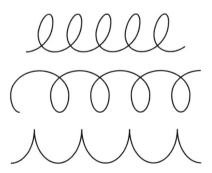

Figure 4.1 Examples of flowing patterns.

to control the pencil and gauge the correct amount of strength that is required. An alternative strategy is to wrap foam round the stem for this can help placement of the fingers if they tend to go too near or far from the point. The thickness of the foam can be reduced as control is gained and as the children become able to select the correct amount of pressure.

Soft or hard lead?

A pencil sharp enough to give a good image is needed. It should not tear the paper. A soft lead (B or 2B) helps those who do not press hard enough and mistakes are easily rubbed out. On the other hand an HB lead is best for children who press too hard, because this kind of lead withstands more pressure before breaking. (See also hypo- and hypersensitivity discussed in Chapter 3.)

Poor strength and faint writing

If the children are having difficulties, it is vitally important to assess the strength the children have in their hands, arms and shoulders. Poor strength will impact on posture that in turn affects balance, control and therefore legibility of the piece of writing. Teachers should look out for poor co-contraction, i.e. the inability to stabilise a joint by contracting the muscles around it. In writing the shoulder muscles need to hold the arm steady so that the wrist and fingers can move independently. Lack of stability results in spidery writing which shows lack of control.

Activities to develop strength in the small muscles in the hand

Note. Developing strength requires some resistance so the plasticine or other moulding material should be firm enough to provide this without being so hard it is not malleable at all.

The activities listed below are useful for developing strength in the small muscles in the hand.

- Moulding plasticine or clay, building sandcastles, playing the piano (an old piano where the keys offer some resistance is best), squeezing a cat's rubber ball and shaking it to make the bell inside sound.

- Drawing through several layers of paper with carbon in between. The child writes then sees how far the pattern has pressed through. This is a multi-sensory experience, the children's vision helping their tactile (feeling) sense. They can easily see the effect of their actions and recognise whether they need to alter their pressure.

■ Making scribble patterns gradually larger (for those who tend to have tiny writing) and gradually smaller (for those children whose writing is too large). These can go straight along the page at first then make 'hills and hollows' to mirror writing shapes.

■ Any sort of climbing frame activity where the arms pull the body up can be strengthening (the muscles have to work hard). Perhaps best of all swimming can strengthen because the water provides a manageable amount of resistance to the shoulders, arms and hands while supporting the rest of the body.

The necessary movement abilities

Crossing the midline of the body

Careful observations can show whether children have difficulty crossing the midline of the body for this competence is part of many everyday coping skills. However, children may well develop strategies to help them overcome this difficulty, e.g. changing the pencil from one hand to the other, or turning the body rather than stretching across. Close observation is required because these strategies do not help in the longer term. Children who cannot cross the midline are limited to working on one side only. This can develop bilateral integration problems when using each hand to do a different part of a combined task is necessary. Skills such as tying laces, spreading butter on bread, using a knife and fork, in fact many of the activities of daily living are hampered by this midline difficulty. Sometimes a key sign can be the children's inability to use the assisting hand to secure the paper when writing or to stretch out the arm to assist balance in gross motor skills.

Poor ocular-motor control at the midline

When the eyes should be smoothly transversing the page, some children experience a visual blip at the midline. This will cause them to skip a word or a line or when reading to lose their place in the text. If these blips happen, those observing should carefully note 'how often' and 'when' and pass this information to the parents with advice to take the child to an optician. Coloured lenses may solve the difficulty for some children.

Enough spatial/kinaesthetic competence

Poor spacing is a common feature of children's writing. Many are advised to put their finger between words to prevent them running together. Another strategy is for each child to have a piece of well-spaced writing as a model (Kiely,1996) and have the difference, i.e. to their own cramped writing, pointed out. Copying from the board can defeat good intentions if tracking abilities are not well developed so any text which has to be copied should lie alongside the lined paper. Coloured marks on both can helpfully indicate starting places. All of these considerations are worthwhile as well-spaced writing does make such a difference to the appearance and legibility of a piece of work.

Lined paper

Most schools now issue blank paper so that children at different developmental stages (often reflected in size preference in their writing) can be accommodated. A second hope is that their thoughts will not be constrained by trying to make their writing fit the lines. With practice and through observation of the work of other children, most gradually adapt to producing writing of an appropriate size.

When children have difficulty regulating the size of letters or remembering L → R directions, however, lined paper helps them structure their work. If all the other children use unlined paper, providing guidelines which shine through from underneath can help children without making them different. Sometimes children are given large sheets of paper to encourage them to make larger drawings or write more words; however some may find this inhibiting or overwhelming.

Stars to begin

'Starting stars' can help children recognise where to begin each letter (see Figure 4.2), and if these are used consistently they can prevent the confusion which commonly arises over b and d. Hornsby (1984) advises teaching letters in 'similar groups' as many writing experts do. She stresses the starting place and offers some advice to prevent the confusion which often arises with 'b'. and 'd'. She explains:

> I have yet to meet a child who reverses 'h', so this is a good letter to start with when teaching 'b'. Even when using cursive writing, the children should concentrate on the starting point to prevent reversals.

As different schemes are developed, the 'best way to teach handwriting' changes and different experts prefer 'beginning with print', 'beginning with cursive writing' or a modified version of it from the start, 'beginning with capitals' or alternatively with small case letters. Teachers within particular schools will probably have to conform to an accepted policy so that there is continuity throughout the classes. Each scheme will have its own rationale, so some brief points are all that is required here.

Figure 4.2 Examples of letters with starting stars.

Beginning with capitals

Most children can draw straight lines and circles before they come to school and so they can manage the capital letters more easily than the smaller case letters. In the early years they can make them as big as they wish, perhaps using sugar paper and they can soon recognise their name by the starting capital letter. However, capital letters often stand alone and some teachers fear that teaching them first will delay the idea of letters flowing together to make a word. In this mode 'when to use the capitals' has to be taught quite soon and this change of usage and the fact that different shaped letters make the same sound can be difficult for young children to understand.

Print or manuscript

The lower case letters are sometimes taught as ball and stick letters that are written one at a time with the pencil lifted in between. Many schools have jettisoned this method because 'joined up' or cursive writing, which eventually must take its place, has to be relearned as another technique.

Some older children with writing difficulties, however, have tried a cursive script and have been relieved to abandon it. Often this has been when a strange pencil grip (which is too late to change) inhibits any natural flow. Having said that, some youngsters can build up a surprising speed that lets them get tasks and assignments finished in time. Later, computers can take over. This may not be thought ideal in some schools but it is a coping strategy and sometimes one that has to suffice. Children with dyspraxia can have a tremendous sense of relief that they can produce legible work that shows what they can do.

Cursive script

Print is upright with vertical lines and circles whereas a cursive script has oval forms and uprights that lean slightly forward. This helps flow, continuity and speed. It also helps word spacing. The kinaesthetic sense can then help internalise the shape of whole words rather than discrete letters. Some individual letters, however, can be more difficult to scribe and component parts have to be carefully taught before building them up into the complete letter forms.

The correct resources

The writing table and chair

First of all the chair must be at the correct height. Children have to be enabled to sit well balanced with their feet securely on the floor. If feet are left dangling, then the children have to shift their position to feel secure or concentrate on balancing in their chair. All this takes away from the attention needed to write. The writing desk should also be at the correct height in relation to the chair. The shoulders should be able to be in a normal relaxed position, not raised and tense in an effort to reach the writing surface. Arms should be resting at right angles on the desk and the back should be straight. Eyes should look down comfortably, without any unnatural head turning to the side.

Inclined writing boards

Inclined boards help many children, especially if copying from the board is required. These should be large enough to stretch well beyond the size of the paper that should in turn be fixed in position with tape so that keeping it in place does not become an added chore. The boards mean the eyes can follow the text more easily because the head does not have to be lifted and lowered.

Enough space on the desktop

The position of the paper in relation to the writer can facilitate or hamper progress. The paper should be on the same side of the body as the writing hand. It should be slanted (for right handers to the left and vice versa for left-handed children) and the other hand should rest on the paper to steady it.

The Anything Left-Handed shop in London gives advice about all aspects of how teachers and parents can help left-handed children. They can be contacted at *www.anythingleft-handed.co.uk*, and a video is also available.

Seating arrangements

Recognition of the space each child needs may have repercussions for the seating plan within the class. A left-handed child sitting to the right of a right-handed one is likely to mean that both are cramped so if space is limited then considering 'right or left handedness' is very important.

Summary of correct resources

- A desk or table and chair at the correct height
- Enough space so that the writing arm can move freely
- A pencil grip which suits each child's hand
- Lined paper to help spacing
- A sloping board to prevent too much leaning over the table and help tracking
- A clear uninterrupted view of the board
- Spatial aids, e.g. starting stars to show where different letters and numbers begin

Left-handed writers

Quite apart from careful seating arrangements left-handed children need specific guidance both in holding their pencil and in the direction they write. If they do not have this support they are likely to develop the hook handwriting position. This is where the hand holding the pencil curves over the top of the writing. The children may be trying to prevent their hand smudging their work. Smudging does occur if the hand has to follow the writing line (in the right-handed child the hand moves away from rather than on top of the text). Avoiding this may cause the left-handed child to cramp his writing arm and hand which makes writing very tiring.(Again, the Anything Left-Handed shop is a good source of advice – contact *www.anythingleft-handed.co.uk*.)

Mirror writing

Left-handed children will naturally want to work across the page from right to left. Often they can produce perfect mirror script as Leonardo da Vinci did. Adjusting the slope of the paper and having a pen which has a left-handed nib can allow the children to concentrate on the 'proper' direction. Pens and pencils with slippery barrels should be avoided because they encourage the children to grip too tightly.

Some tips for supporting left-handed children (supplied by The Left-Handers Club, 5 Charles Street, Worcester WR1 2AQ (*www.lefthand-education. co.uk*)) include:

- Ask the child to hold the pencil at least 2 cm away from the tip so that they do not obscure their writing.

- Provide a soft pencil that does not tear the paper.

- Provide stars to help the children know where to begin.

- Correct the angle of the paper. This should lie to the left of the midline of the body with the top tilted at an angle of 45°. This should ensure that the hand could stay comfortably underneath the writing line.

- Left-handed children should be seated on the left side of a double desk or table or next to another left-handed child. This saves elbows coming together and each writer being cramped.

- To encourage lighter writing, placing carbon paper between sheets of paper and asking the child to write without making a mark below can be helpful and fun!

Shannon and Dionne show how much space they need to accommodate their different writing hands. Both hands are below the script.

Dionne (LH) and Josh (RH) tackle cutting out from different directions.

Note. The teacher should be able to demonstrate the letters showing where the left-handed children start each one. Watching the children cutting out circles can reveal how they will use different directions.

Many of these considerations apply to mathematics too.

Mathematics

Numbers can be exciting, challenging tools or the source of great anxiety. Mathematics is a subject that depends on organisation and patterns (Ashcroft and Chinn, 1992). Children have therefore to be able to recognise these patterns and manipulate shapes to make others. Such feats rely heavily on movement competences such as visual acuity, clear spatial perception and fine motor skills. All the difficulties implicit in handwriting skills may also impact on the formation of numbers, while poor reading ability may prevent success when problems are set out in text rather than diagrams. Even using a calculator requires deft finger movements so any wrong answer may be due to inability to hit the correct key rather than misunderstanding the calculation.

Studying workbooks on early mathematics highlights just how much competent movement contributes to success. Consider some of these requests:

1. Cut out the sweets and place them in the jar.

2. Cut out the cars and place them in the car park.

3. Draw 1 apple.

4. Ring the correct number.

5. Count on your fingers up to 5.

6. Lay out the counters in the table.

The children need control of their writing hand and arm if they are to fulfil these requests, and for the last they need both hand awareness and dexterity which includes the ability to let go, a more sophisticated competence than grasping or picking up the counters.

A progression on this basic work asks the children to recognise groups of objects by the pattern they make rather than by counting them out. Questions such as, 'How many are there?' require the children to recognise patterns, i.e. to make visual–spatial judgements. At first they can touch the objects, perhaps pulling them to one side as they count, but soon they have to recognise the pattern and identify the number without touching – quite a demanding feat for those who do not see patterns easily or for those who have not achieved conservation, i.e. the ability to realise that changing the shape of a pattern leaves its number value intact.

Conservation

Piaget claimed that children were not capable of conservation before the age of 7. More recent studies have claimed that, if child-friendly language is used in a context that the children understand, many younger ones can cope with the idea that rearranging amounts – of water or counters or lengths of pathways – does not change their intrinsic 'value'.

However, if children are prompted through having explanations then teachers have to be sure that the underlying concepts have been understood. If not, more difficult calculations such as subtraction and transfer of learning will not have a firm base.

Visual perception

Children with visual difficulties may see the numbers move on the page just as the letters in their reading books do. Coloured overlays can help keep the numbers still. Of course children with this difficulty may not realise that all children do not see the same things and so not share their problem with their parents or their teacher. In many children with dyslexia, the visual processing apparatus of the brain distorts the images seen by the eye (de Buitleir, 2003). Writing numbers can be the first point of confusion. Children often write 3 reversed and/or mix it with 8, or confuse 6 with 9, or read 3 as 5, but often this rights itself if repeated patient explanations are given and pre-counting activities, e.g. songs and rhymes, are revisited.

Differentiating between the symbols +, x and ÷ may also cause problems. Some children will stay with an original operation even after the operational sign has been changed. They lack the flexibility in interchanging signs. Visual perceptual difficulties may be present.

Sequencing difficulties

In most arithmetical operations, the children must be able to sequence, i.e. they must remember the order of what to do first, then next. Children who do not visualise patterns easily can find retaining the order of several digits and how they should be manipulated very tricky.

Counting on the number track

The number track gives a visual picture of counting forwards and backwards and the children learn to count to 5 and back and to then to 10 and back. The progression asks them to begin at different places and to count up and down the line (see Figure 4.3). They then have to find which is 'one more than' or 'one less than' and so internalise that moving to the right means more. This is early practice in directionality and can be difficult for children with poor hand dominance or awareness of laterality.

The difficulty is exacerbated when place value is introduced for then the direction of increased value changes (see Figure 4.4).

Figure 4.3 The number line – value increases to the right.

Figure 4.4 Place value – value increases to the left.

Children are also asked to count/track moving numbers

Just as in reading the words on a page, tracking skills are needed here. If the children's eyes jump over numbers, they are going to find it impossible to give an accurate reply. The number track is a powerful model that helps children with abstraction, i.e. moving from working with concrete materials to being able to count forwards and backwards according to pictures in their heads. It must be recognised, however, that while most children need to begin handling materials, some prefer to use abstract thinking and may feel hampered by having to refer to a track or manipulate materials.

Moving from the track to the number line

This progression involves a shift in spatial orientation because, whereas the track consisted of blocks representing quantities (i.e. three-dimensional representation), the number line is two-dimensional. Many children find it difficult to make the shift.

Spatial understanding in different algorithms

Some children have great difficulty lining up their work even when squared paper is provided. If the columns and rows confuse them, then their work will be incorrectly set out defeating any mathematical skill in producing the correct answer.

The inconsistent starting points of the different sorts of arithmetical computations can also be very difficult to remember. In addition the children start at the right-hand side and move to the left, while in division the children start at the left and move to the right. In subtraction the child starts at the bottom right but has to remember to 'take' the lower number from the top one, 'borrow' from the left upper digit and then move left. It is not difficult to see why children with visual perception and/or spatial orientation problems are confused. To cope children have to be sure of directions, especially right and left. Many movement activities can help this (see Chapter 5).

Children with visual processing difficulties may find it difficult to differentiate between numbers and symbols, e.g. 6 and 9 or 3 and 8 or + and ×. If they store the incorrect image in their memory then this causes them to form the number poorly. They may also read it as one digit but write it as another (de Buitleir, 2003).

Mental maths

'Mental maths' holds many hurdles for children with poor short-term or working memories. In this area of maths the children often have to find the correct answer then hold the correct number aloft or sort a plastic fan of numbers so that the correct answer is isolated from the rest. Quite apart from the difficulty in remembering the sum when all this sorting is required, the choice of number has to be made by moving the resource quickly. Inability to do this in time can stress a child with poor fine motor skills. Inability to do this may confuse the teacher into thinking that the child does not know the correct answer when this may not be the case.

The confusing language of mathematics

Unfortunately mathematics has different terms to describe the same operation. 'Subtract', 'take away', 'minus', 'what is the difference', 'how much less than', all indicate subtraction. How confusing this is for children with language processing difficulties (Sharma, 1990). The 8-year-olds meet polysyllabic words, e.g. multiplication and equilateral triangle. While many children love to master this language it can be perplexing for children with dyslexia, dyspraxia and those with speech and language difficulties.

Overlying all of these problems is the strong influence of the children's self-concept. If they believe they cannot do maths, this soon translates into hating maths or being afraid to go to maths. Unfortunately this can become a cycle of despair–anxiety influencing perception and motor competence leading to more wrong answers – and the cycle goes on.

Despite all of these possibilities, however, many children with and without specific learning difficulties love maths. Many dyslexic children claim that it is their favourite subject. Perhaps this is because problems can be expressed in symbols rather than words. However, 60 per cent of children with specific learning difficulties do have difficulties with maths, as do very many others (Chinn and Ashcroft, 1993). Given the range of possible difficulties outlined here, parents and teachers have to remember that a wrong answer may have a different source – it may not really mean that the mathematical computation has been misunderstood! Budding mathematicians must not be held back by movement difficulties. The underlying competences must be addressed first!

CHAPTER 5

Programmes of activities for perceptual-movement programmes

Introduction

There are many activities throughout the book that can be substituted or added to the ones suggested here. Each activity in this section is given as a developmental sequence so that those who decide on the content of the programmes can chose the level of input that is appropriate for the group of children they are working with. Selecting from the range of gross motor, fine motor and manipulative skills will ensure coverage of all the basic movement patterns. It is important that the children are involved in the planning of the daily activity session, either in deciding and then telling what it is they want to do, or in recapping what they did. This develops two skills: the first ensures that the children learn the language of movement and shows if they can make appropriate plans; the second helps keep the movement pattern in the memory, so that can be used as feedback for subsequent tries. The discussion also helps the selection and organisation of resources.

Teachers preparing a programme have to remember that, very often, it is the planning and organising aspect of movement that is the most difficult and that concentrating on 'remembering' and 'helping children to use feedback to improve the next try' is critically important. This 'intellectual' side of movement is often left aside because adults take it for granted that the children will know what they are doing and remember what they did beyond the lesson itself. Many children with specific learning difficulties, however, don't remember without extra repetition and sustained practice. Poor memory also prevents them from using feedback so checking this is as important as the children being able to 'do' the movements themselves. Sometimes children enjoy recording what they did, e.g. drawing the apparatus, giving themselves a star or recording their score telling how well they thought they did. All these help reinforcement and the retention of the movement till it becomes habitual.

Exercise 1

Activity to help remembering and planning

1. Provide a variety of apparatus, which includes the apparatus from 'yesterday', e.g. a bench, beanbags, hoops and two mats

2. Ask the child to help set out the pattern of apparatus 'which he used last time' and then ask him to 'show what you did so well'. Remind and revisit the sequence as necessary, remembering to reinforce the quality descriptors, e.g. sink down very slowly, then make your back round as a ball as you roll on the mat, etc.

3. When the child has remembered and practised, add some other resources and invite the child to make a new sequence. Ask 'What would you like to do?' and be ready with a simple suggestion (perhaps two ideas) if he doesn't know. If he agrees, let him try, giving reminders when necessary. Repeat till secure.

4. Praise the child, then ask: 'Would you like to show a friend how well you can do this?' This means repeating the activity but with the added difficulty of showing someone else.

5. Immediately, the child should draw the sequence. Reinforce the planning words:

> First you did,… and next came…till last of all…

The child can write the action words underneath each part of the picture.

Note. The child is not being asked to solve a problem someone else has devised. The critical learning is being able to remember what was done before, to devise a new but similar plan and to be able to follow it through.

Progression

1. Ask the child, 'Would you like to change one part of your sequence?' Or if this is too difficult, 'Would you like to change the first part?' (Changing the first part is less stressful.)

2. Discuss how this will affect the order of the movements. Write or draw the new sequence.

3. Add another piece of apparatus, e.g. a tunnel or a box.

4. Repeat the same format – emphasising 'first', 'next', and 'last of all'.

It is important that every opportunity is taken to have children learn the language of movement. Such words can then be used subsequently as a more complex lesson plan is taught and the teacher need not interrupt a demonstration or an explanation to remind the children, say, what 'feel your balance' or 'think about your landing' means. It is also important that children learn directional words, e.g. through, under then over, beside and beyond, because these will feature regularly in many activities beyond movement per se, e.g. in mathematics and junior science. Some activities have names, e.g. star jump, forward or pencil roll, bunny jump, bounce pass, etc. and if these are used regularly as suggestions for change or as reminders of key points, e.g. 'remember to stretch out every part of your body right down to your toes in your pencil roll', then the children soon build a visual picture of what they are aiming for. 'Instructions' have to be brief as movement is over in a flash.

Six golden rules

Before starting out, there are six golden rules to remember:

1. Safety first

Keep the children safe. As a few children will attempt things beyond their capability, those in charge must know the children and their level of movement competence before introducing any climbing or balancing apparatus. Practioners also have to ensure that all apparatus is securely fixed and that there are enough thick mats to cushion all possible falls.

2. Teach the children how to land

As soon as possible, teach the children to land safely. This means they have to learn about resilience or the 'spring in their knees' which helps absorb their weight on landing then pushes them up again. They also have to learn how to roll safely, i.e. to tuck in the 'jagged bits' such as heads, knees and elbows so that the more cushioned areas, such as the back of their shoulders and hips, take the impact on any landing or rolling. Landings can be practised from a crawling position, then from standing then from jumping down from a low bench.

3. Begin with simple movements and ensure that they are done well

There is no mystery – all movement is beneficial if it is carefully taught in sequential steps. Standing and walking well is an important goal for all children because, even in these simple patterns, moving with confidence can help them to feel a sense of poise, to feel good and so lose their inhibitions in tackling new things. Programmes can be based on the activities of everyday living, e.g. stepping onto different heights of steps at walking speed then more quickly, or practising tying laces, doing up zips or packing a bag, because these things are possibly going to be the most useful of all. To do them successfully the children need to have the necessary strength, balance and co-ordination and they have to understand how each skill depends on an underlying plan.

4. Praise individual effort as well as improvement and progress

Avoid competition unless it is a 'beating your own score' type of activity. Competition introduces hurrying that causes fluster and stress. The movement itself then deteriorates. Furthermore, in a large game, most young children would not have enough turns of the ball, nor would they be able to follow the rules. Individual practice or practices in twos is best in the early years.

5. Use every chance to observe and assess

Everything that happens can be planned to give diagnostic material leading to dynamic assessment. For example, I purposely gave a 9-year-old child a blunt pencil to record his own score. Watching him sharpen it gave me the opportunity to see if his 'working at the midline of the body' had improved – without him realising that he was being observed or assessed.

6. Provide opportunities for recap

Lots of 'helping to put out the beanbags' or 'giving out bands' responsibilities are important in giving the children time to anticipate what is about to happen as well as the confidence gained through being chosen to help. These are subtle observational opportunities not to be missed!

Fun ways of teaching

All the activities can be taught using jingles because these give a lively input, they help the rhythm and the short-term memory and they allow practice of the basic movement patterns. For example:

> Crawl through the grass
> Be small, small, small.
> Tuck your toes and knees in
> And roll into a ball.
>
> Reach up to the roof now,
> Stretch up very high.
> Are you on your tiptoes?
> Can you touch the sky?
>
> Stand up very well now,
> Shake your shoulders down.
> March around the room now,
> Be the smartest ones in town!

Some ideas for content suitable for perceptual-motor programmes follow. Some teaching possibilities are shared to show that teaching points are quite straightforward if they are based on an analysis of each movement pattern.

Exercise 2

Crawling – a critically important gross motor skill

Crawling should be part of every movement session. This is because of the balance, co-ordination and spatial orientation it promotes in addition to the cross lateral patterning. Able children (in movement terms) can crawl up inclined benches and through clear tunnels so that the activity retains enough challenge. Children with movement/specific learning difficulties can find crawling impossible, so games in the crawling position without moving from the spot can help establish the table position and a gentle change of weight.

Amy, in the crawling (prone kneeling) position, is throwing a beanbag into a bucket. The shift in weight necessary to stretch and pick up the beanbag and the adjustment needed to move from four balance points to three is important. The activity lets her experience being slightly off-balance and then finding the point of regaining balance again. She also has to learn to make the correct spatial choices e.g. how far? in what direction? how do I adjust my body to let that kind of movement happen?

Points to check

■ *Balance and strength*:

   – As one arm is lifted, how secure is the weight shift from four points to three?
   – Can the children stay strong or do the three limbs supporting the body weight collapse?
   – Can the children readjust their position once the arm comes back?
   – As the head is lifted or lowered does the body swing back over the feet? If so go back to help the children feel their body parts in the table position and give them support as the weight shifts onto three limbs.

■ *Hand dominance.* Do the children use the same hand to toss the beanbag into the bin? This shows if they have developed hand dominance. If they are unsure or keep changing hands, ask them to decide 'which hand gets most winners.' This can help hand dominance to be established.

As soon as the children get three beanbags into the bin they can move further back so that their throw needs more strength and accuracy. Rings around the bin can be used to score points (see Figure 5.1).

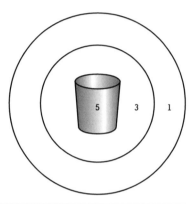

Figure 5.1 Target practice to reveal hand dominance.

Note. Avoid keeping the children kneeling for too long as this practice can be tiring for those that lack strength in their arms or legs.

Progression

Wag the tail of the dog

From the basic crawling/table position, the children have to stretch one leg out behind and then wave it to show they are pleased. Little ones love to respond in this way when their teacher tells them how special they are or that they have done well. They should try to sustain the strength in their arms, keep their backs flat and not collapse forward. Very brief attempts with either leg are best. Again it can be useful to see which leg children extend first and if this is the same one they use for kicking a ball.

Children with poor kinaesthetic/proprioceptive awareness will twist to look at their leg as they don't have a clear 'feeling picture' of what is happening. They need lots of body awareness practices, e.g. rubbing knees, stamping feet – perhaps done to jingles, for example:

A *hand awareness jingle:*

Put your hands on your shoulders

And hands on your knees

Clap them…and shake them…

And give them a squeeze.

Now push them up into the air

And hold them very high,

Look to see the shape they make,

Like stars up in the sky.

Hold your arms wide open now

And make them spin you round,

Gently sink and curl right up

And tuck into the ground.

Tunnels (younger children)

The children in twos take it in turns to roll a ball through the tunnel (forward to back) made by the child holding the prone kneeling position.

Progression

The tunnels line up one behind the other and hold the position till the ball goes through. The child at the back collects the ball and goes to the front while the 'roller' joins the front. There is a great deal of getting up and down and positioning correctly in this game so it is a good idea not to rush the children as they make their moves. Once they have mastered the idea they enjoy shuffling backwards. This is useful as not many activities ask the children to move backwards.

Note. As the children watch the progress of the ball they will look down and through their arms. They should be encouraged to hold the table position rather than allowing their arms or legs to collapse.

Exercise 3

Obstacle courses (interspersing crawling with other movement patterns)

Crawling over mats and benches, through hoops, under ropes, etc. using whatever equipment is available to make an interesting obstacle course provides a good opportunity to establish directional/spatial language and helps balance to be developed while in a safe position.

An obstacle course introduces an uneven terrain so balance and co-ordination adjustments have to be made all the time. Observers should note whether the cross lateral pattern is sustained and any difficulties the children have in getting down into the crawling position and standing up again.

Exercise 4

Kicking horses (older children)

Only when the children show that they can take the weight forward onto their arms safely can they progress to try 'kicking horses'. In this activity, one leg is stretched behind and swung up into the air. This is the preparation for a handstand. Not all children will progress to this.

Points to check

■ The hands should be flat on the floor with fingers spread approximately shoulder width apart.

- The head should be looking up, not through the arms. This helps balance.

- Note which foot is stretched out to see if foot dominance is established.

Exercise 5

Cross lateral movement

The balance needed to hold the limbs steady has to be acquired first. Then the rhythm can be counted out as the pattern is demonstrated.

(If difficulties persist, the child may have a retained primitive reflex that is preventing progress. Specific advice can be obtained from INPP, 4 Stanley Place, Chester CH1 2LU (tel. 01244 311414).)

Exercise 6

Standing still, walking and balancing along benches

Standing still needs balance and control and, for those who find this difficult, attention needs to focus on the symmetrical position of the body about an imaginary midline. (This can tie up with a classroom lesson on symmetry because the visual picture of symmetrical shapes will be established there.) Picturing a line of symmetry drawn on their bodies helps the children understand balance (keeping two sides equal). It also helps children to be aware of crossing the midline in the plethora of activities of daily living where this has to happen. Helpful teaching input might include the following:

1. Feel both soles of your feet on the floor. Push down and make them both strong.

2. Where are your knees? Can you feel them facing forward? Are they both keeping your legs straight?

3. Are your hips facing forward? Put your hands on your hips so that they don't turn to the side.

4. Check now – toes, knees and hips all facing forward?

5. Think about your shoulders now. Shrug them up to your ears and let them flop down. Make sure they feel quite easy, not tense at all.

Are your thumbs by the side of your legs? Swing your arms gently and make them still again. Can you still feel where they are?

6. Now think about your head. Are you facing forward? Are you steady? Can you feel the top of your head? Can you feel each ear?

7. Do you feel balanced and ready to move now? Good, let's go!

This could seem like using a hammer to crack a nut but once the routine is internalised, it just takes a moment to ask the children to 'be steady and get your balance before you move'. As the questions are asked the children are developing their body awareness, which is fundamental to safe movement. It is important that the children feel how to be well poised before and during movement. They also need to understand how to regain a balanced (safe) position if moving, e.g. pencil rolling over a mat, has temporarily disorientated them.

Exercise 7

Walking

As this movement pattern is the basis of many others and as poised walking is healthy (it encourages deep breathing and so invigorates the body), it should be built into many games. The points emphasised in standing well should be revisited. The shoulders should be relaxed, not tense. This can be helped by the arms swinging naturally in opposition to the leg action. The foot action should be a transfer of weight from the heel to the toe to aid propulsion. (Check that the soles of the children's shoes are not too stiff to let this happen.)

Walking well practices

Use dramatic ideas to help the children understand how non-verbals communicate the meaning of an action. For example, ask the children to do the following:

- Walk to a spot at the other side of the room. Can you feel the top of your head? (The head should be held naturally, without strain.)

- Walk to greet a friend who has just come back from hospital and is feeling very well. Shake hands kindly.

- Walk to tell another friend that their football team has lost an important match. Shake hands sadly.

Discuss the body position (open and closed shoulders, the speed of the walking action) in the three events. This helps body awareness and communication skills as the children learn to interpret non-verbal cues. This is especially important for children who find making friends diffi-cult. In this kind of activity the children also learn that other people are reading their body language. This can be developed in drama lessons too by asking the children to convey different messages without talking.

A further activity could be as follows:

■ Limit the space and have the children to walk around each other (accompanied by tambourine jingles). Use a rhythmical sequence, e.g. scamper and scamper and scamper and freeze, melt to the floor and bounce up again.

Activities like this mean the children have to be aware of their body alignment and appreciate how much space their body uses. They also have to change direction on a jagged or curved pathway. Some children will tense up because they do not enjoy proximity. Being over-protective of personal space could be a sign of a tactile difficulty (see Chapter 2). If this is observed, do the same activity but have small groups of children. In this way they will still have the experience of changing direction and controlling the balance and pace of their movement, but the spatial ten-sion will be removed.

Marching, halting and 'right/left turn'

Many children enjoy playing at soldiers and while it is not necessary for them to achieve the over-rigidity of the soldiers' march, they do have a mental image of important people walking well and enjoy being like them. Having children marching and changing direction stimulates good body and spatial awareness as well as being the source of new words, e.g. follow, halt, stand easy, attention, left turn, right turn. They also learn to anticipate changes of direction. Dragging out the first word, e.g. 'riiiiiight turn', helps this!

Walking along a bench

The bench must be steady, for wobbles can deter some insecure children from trying altogether. Practitioners can hold one hand gently for a first try. It is also a good idea to have the bench in a quiet spot so that tenta-tive children don't worry about being jostled off. The children should stand well balanced before they begin else they will use too much strength to get onto the bench and this throws them off balance. They should be encouraged to walk well looking ahead when they can. Having beanbags as obstacles adds interest but it also means the children tend to look down so this has to be considered in relation to what has to be achieved.

Once these movement patterns are established most children seem to gain confidence but there should always be enough variety in the arrangement of any apparatus to provide scope for the able children (in movement terms) and those who need a great deal of support (see Figure 5.2).

In any arrangement the climbing apparatus, the balancing benches and the jumping down possibilities should have two levels of challenge. This means that all the children can be busy while building up their skill. The spatial arrangement is important too. Mats should be sufficiently thick to cushion any falls and approach runs and landing areas should be planned so that the children will not run into or fall over each other.

Strengthening legs

Real difficulties, that is where lack of strength is impairing the child's lifestlye, need specialist and immediate physiotherapy help. Children can practise the following:

- Stepping up stairs.
- Stepping onto and off benches, trying to sustain a rhythm.
- Sitting, arms behind the body (strongly supporting) with legs stretched up held slightly (15 cm) off the ground. The children can try one leg at a time first.
- Sitting facing a partner. Holding a beanbag between two feet and tossing it back and forward to each other.

Exercise 8

Helping balance

What else can be done to help develop a sense of balance?

1. Gentle movements, e.g. low swinging or sitting astride then rocking on a rocking horse, or walking on dry sand or over an uneven surface can give practice in sustaining control. The children should

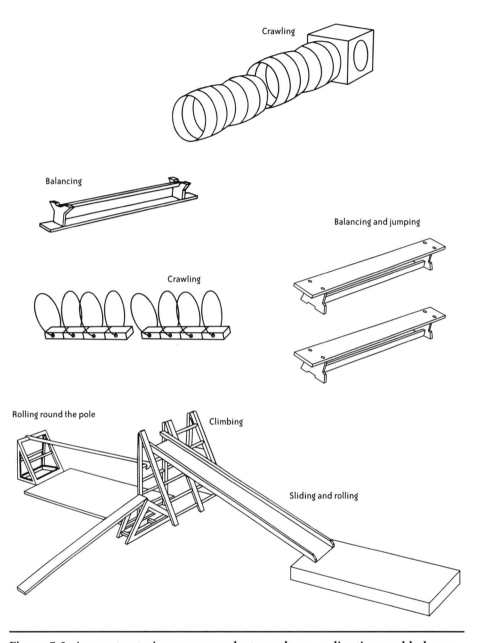

Figure 5.2 Apparatus to improve speed, strength, co-ordination and balance.

always feel safe and in charge of increasing the arc of the swing or the rocking action or the length of time they walk on uneven paths.

2. All the swing park activities that seem to be out of favour today are excellent in providing opportunities to develop movement skills. Moreover, the children are in charge of what they want to do and can plan activities to suit their level of confidence and competence.

3. Swimming is excellent for both strengthening and developing a sense of balance as the water supports the body while providing some resistance. The children should be encouraged to keep both sides of the body the same, for example in feeling the feet coming together in breast stroke or in stretching out on both sides equally while floating (holding onto the grab rail if necessary). Quite apart from the safety aspect, being able to swim is a wonderful achievement. It gives the children's self-esteem a useful boost.

4. Pushing along the ground with both feet while securely seated on a tricycle is another good practice for the children can feel the effect of pushing too hard with one foot while still being supported and being able to retrieve a balanced position.

5. Careful walking along the broad side of a bench requires quite a number of spatial and balance decisions to be made, especially if turning around at the end to walk back or stepping over obstacles is part of the task. Such planning decisions involves:

   - the amount of strength needed to step up and hold a balanced position;
   - how to position the feet – children who find balancing difficult should pause with two feet together to feel a balanced position before walking on;
   - how much speed to use – children tend to want to get to the other end too quickly and this may throw their balance;
   - when to lift one foot to step over the obstacle and how high to lift the foot;
   - when to begin the turn around and how to organise the foot pattern in the turn.

Many children will need time to practise and this is best done in a quiet area away from other children rushing around because this can distract them and spoil their concentration. Children who do not wish to attempt this can walk along a line on the floor.

Note. Some schools have bought very short benches probably considering that this makes the task easier. Unfortunately the children are often planning to get off before they have felt the poise of a balanced walk so unfortunately this well-intentioned purchase can defeat the point of the exercise.

Progression

For children who find walking along a bench easy then asking them to carry a hoop above their head or roll a ball around their body as they move along can add challenge without having to change the apparatus. If there are two benches available, of course, one bench can be turned upside down so that the walking is on the narrow side.

Exercise 9

Balancing on different parts of the body

A practice which helps both body awareness and balance is to have the children experiment and find different body parts on which they can balance. The variety is endless and most importantly the children can select and define their own level of challenge. The teacher might like to suggest that the children 'try to balance on small bits – or one large and one small part'. This makes the children think about the way the size of their base affects their balance. Some choices might be:

■ one foot and one hand (suggest on the same side of the body as well as cross-over balances);

■ balance on hips, arms tucked round knees;

■ balance on the back of shoulders, legs stretched up in the air;

■ two hands and one knee, one hand and one knee (provide mats);

■ lying on one side – other leg up in the air;

■ two hands and two feet to make a bridge.

The little ones like to make a bridge for a mouse, perhaps just using finger and thumb, and one for an elephant to go through, using two arms and two legs!

Exercise 10

Running

In running the arms should help the propulsion of the action. This is best practised outside to give a feeling of distance to be covered and therefore a real purpose in using the arms. If the children have been taught to walk and march, they should be used to feeling a balanced position as they move.

Walking, running and changing direction

Some children manage a curved pathway but cannot make abrupt changes of direction. If this difficulty is observed, the position of the feet should be checked. If the toes turn in then the knees and hips will be turning in too and the child needs help to make them face forward. Physiotherapy is necessary if improvement is slow. Drawing chalk lines on the grass can provide a simple pathway. Marching games where the children 'obey orders' without using apparatus offers another opportunity for observation.

Running and jumping

At the start, 'jumping' can be over a very low rope so that the running pattern is hardly interrupted. This allows children to establish their preferred take off foot and lets observers see whether foot dominance has been established. When the rope is very low, the momentum of the run need not be broken. The rope should be raised gradually as the children run in a straight line. Only when this is successful should changes of heights and directions be added.

Children who can't jump because they are unsure of the point of take-off may need the rhythm of the pattern explained, perhaps by the teacher calling out, 'run and run, and over you go!' Gradually the children can say the rhythm too so that it is internalised. The length of the approach run should be carefully planned so that the correct take-off foot leads the way and so that enough strength can be gathered for the flight. If the run-up is too short there will not be enough speed to lift the body into a jump, but if it is too long the children may become flustered and/or lose control.

Exercise 11

Catching a ball

This is an important skill because it is the basis of many games and it is a skill highly valued by children.

1. At first, use a balloon with some rice inside. This gives the children more time to position themselves and to gauge the descent of the balloon. The rice makes a little sound to help concentration and tracking and the children know that even if they mis-time the catch they won't be hurt.

2. Using a soft beach ball or volleyball, ensure the ball is thrown sympathetically into a waiting basket (two hands held ready). It may be necessary to call out the rhythm, 'are you ready, Here it comes … catch!

It is important to remember that some children will have difficulty seeing the approaching ball in time to alter the position of the body or hands. To ease this, the area behind the thrower should be as plain as possible. This means that the catcher is not distracted by patterns or movements. As catching is mastered, the distance, the speed and the direction of the thrown ball can be changed.

Exercise 12

Strengthening fingers

Many activities need strong fingers. Strengthening exercises can be disguised easily as part of the curriculum. Examples include:

■ Moulding play-doh, clay or dough for baking. Even making a snowball and patting the shape helps finger control.

■ Threading helps the pincer grip to be developed and this is the basis of the tripod grip for writing.

■ Playing the piano is excellent because of the 'musical' feedback. Scales should be done carefully using the 1, 2, 3, tuck the thumb under method. This encourages the children to watch their fingers and so contributes to body awareness too. Keyboards don't give enough resistance – an old piano is best.

- Picking up and carefully building blocks in the construction corner again provides some resistance to strengthen fingers.

- Lifting jugs of water and pouring from one container to another, controlling the flow provides strengthening work.

- Drawing pictures in wet sand.

- Grasping a bean-ball. This helps strengthen and in giving tactile feedback can help the children to settle down to listen.

- Any squeezing activity, e.g. squirting water from a plastic water gun to paint a pattern on a wall or hit balloons suspended from a washing line. The water makes the gun quite heavy so provides strengthening work for the fingers.

- Using tongs of different shapes and sizes to pick up objects.

- Cutting activities using card to give resistance.

- Outdoors, pulling a cart along in the garden area.

- Any balance activity where the body weight goes forward onto the hands.

- Popping bubble wrap is a favourite one!

Planning and organising movement

Children should always be asked, 'what are you going to do?' and be helped to explain. The order of events or the sequencing may need help and, if so, a 'I am going to do this and then that' scenario can be enough. If the children decide to use resources then they should be involved in choosing and setting them out so that organisation becomes an important part of each task. Collecting them at tidy-up time also reminds them what was done.

The importance of practice

Children constantly surprise by what they can accomplish, especially if they are motivated to keep trying. This is achieved by setting realistic tasks with one set of instructions at a time and offering praise and reminders couched in positive terms.

However, asking the children to practise at the end of the day can be self-defeating and cause resentment when they are tired. The thought of squirting water or popping bubble wrap can often re-energise, however, and even having a small time to practise is better then nothing at all. Practices should be fun and achievement, however small, should be rewarded by a smile, a nod or a sticker just to show that improvement has been recognised and that all the effort on everyone's part has been worthwhile.

Norms of development

Age	Locomotor patterns	Non-locomotor patterns	Manipulative skills
1 month		Supports head. Can lift head from prone lying	Will hold onto object placed in hand
3–4 months		Stepping reflex pattern	Plays with hands as a first toy
5 months	Rolls over from back to front	Holds head and shoulders erect when sitting	Stretches out to grasp with increasing accuracy
6–8 months	Some children begin to crawl	Sits unsupported	Begins to be able to let go
9 months	Can stand with support	Pulls up to stand holding furniture	Transfers objects from one hand to the other
10 months	Crawling established	Can bend to pick up objects when one hand is held	Can use two hands doing different actions at the midline of the body
1 year	Can crawl, stand alone and some children can walk unaided Uses step together pattern to climb stairs	Early walking. Starts games such as peek-boo	Can build bricks, pours water, eats finger food independently Monosyllabic babbling
2 years	Can climb up and down stairs safely now using a passing step pattern	Problem-solving – empties cupboards, dismantles toys	Pulls off clothes. Can put on roomy garments – shoes on wrong feet. Increasing independence
2–3 years	Tries to hop, even skip, but usually uses a galloping pattern. Very immature running and jumping	Enjoys simple lift out puzzles, jigsaws. Mimics others. Wants to make choices and be in charge!	Can lift and pull and push heavier objects Begins to notice what other children are doing Tries to hit ball with bat; little control.
3–4 years	Tries to dress independently. Can manage at the toilet	Can catch large ball. Rides a trike	Early co-operative play Learning to take turns and wait
5 years	Basic movement patterns achieved. Can swim, hop, ride a bike	Enjoys climbing running, immature kicking and other movement patterns	Can form letters and numbers and understand directional language

Competences from the curriculum guidance documents

Emotional, personal and social development	Communication	Knowledge and understanding	Expressive development	Physical development and movement
• Develop confidence, self-esteem and a sense of security	• Have fun with language and making stories	• Develop their powers of observation using their senses	• Investigate and use a variety of media and techniques such as painting, drawing, printing and modelling with fabrics, clay and other materials	• Enjoy energetic activity both indoors and out and the feeling of well-being that it brings
• Care for themselves and their personal safety	• Listen to other children and adults during social activities and play	• Recognise patterns, shapes and colours in the world around them	• Express thoughts and feelings in pictures, paintings and models	• Explore different ways in which they can use their bodies in physical activity
• Develop independence, for example in dressing and personal hygiene	• Listen with enjoyment and respond to stories, songs, music, rhymes and other poetry	• Sort and categorise things into groups	• Use role play or puppets to recreate and invent sutiations	• Use their bodies to express ideas and feelings in response to music and imaginative ideas
• Persevere in tasks that at first present some difficulties	• Listen and respond to the sounds and rhythm of words in stories, songs, music and rhymes	• Understand some properties of materials, for example soft/hard, smooth/rough	• Use verbal and non-verbal language in role play	• Run, jump, skip, climb, balance, throw and catch with increasing skill and confidence
• Express appropriately feelings, needs and preferences	• Pay attention to information and instructions from an adult	• Understand the routines and jobs of familiar people	• Listen and respond to sounds, rhythms, songs and a variety of music	• Co-operate with others in physical play and games
• Form positive relationships with other children and adults, and begin to develop particular friendships with other children	• Talk to other children or with an adult about themselves and their experiences	• Become familiar with the early years setting and places in the local area	• Make music by singing, clapping and playing percussion instruments	• Develop increasing control of the fine movements of their fingers and hands
		• Become aware of everyday uses of technology and use these appropriately (scissors, waterproof clothing, fridge, bicycle)		

- Become aware of and respect the needs and feelings of others in their behaviour, and learn to follow rules
- Make and express choices, plans and decisions
- Play co-operatively, take turns and share resources
- Become aware that the celebration of cultural and religious festivals are important
- Develop positive attitudes towards others whose gender, language, religion or culture, for example, is different from their own.
- Care for the environment and for other people in the community

- Express needs, thoughts and feelings with increasing confidence in speech and non-verbal language
- Take part in short and more extended conversations
- Use talk during role play and re-tell a story or rhyme
- Use language for a variety of purposes, for example to describe, explain, predict, ask questions and develop ideas
- Use books to find interesting information
- Recognise the link between the written and spoken word
- Understand some of the language and layout of books
- Develop an awareness of letter names and sounds in the context of play experiences
- Use their own drawings and written marks to express ideas and feelings
- Experiment with symbols, letters and, in some cases, words in writing
- Recognise some familiar words and letters, for example the initial letter in their name

- Be aware of daily time sequences and words to describe/measure time, for example snack-time, morning, first, next, clock
- Be aware of change and its effects on them, for example their own growth, changes in weather, trees, flowers
- Care for living things, for example, pets at home
- Be aware of feeling good and of the importance of hygiene, diet, exercise and personal safety
- Develop an appreciation of natural beauty and a sense of wonder about the world
- Understand and use mathematical processes such as matching, grouping, counting and measuring
- Apply these processes in solving mathematical problems
- Identify and use numbers up to ten during play experiences and counting games
- Recognise familiar shapes during play activities
- Use mathematical language appropriate to the learning situations

- Use instruments by themselves and in groups to invent music that expresses their thoughts and feelings
- Move rhythmically and expressively to music
- Participate in simple dances and singing games

- Develop awareness of space
- Be safe in movement and in using tools and equipment
- Be aware of the importance of health and fitness

Source: HMI (1997).

The underlying factors influencing movement

Movement abilities
Balance
Co-ordination
Rhythm and timing
Strength and speed

Physical abilities
Growth – body build, height and weight
Maturation
Readiness
Disability

Intellectual abilities
Knowing what to do
Being able to plan ahead
*Being able to organise self
    and resources*

Social and personal development
Able to communicate
Able to hold eye contact
Able to work in groups
Able to lead/follow as needed

Movement

Emotional/temperamental traits
Impulsive – Reflective
Vulnerable – Resilient
Confident – Low self-esteem

Neurological development
Myelination primitive/postural reflexes
Memory (short and long term)
Habituation

ppendix 4

A brief outline of specific learning difficulties

As the conditions or syndromes ADHD, ADD, dyspraxia and dyslexia have been referred to in the text, this appendix offers a brief outline of each. As knowledge about each grows, the overlap of distinguishing factors becomes more evident, so readers who observe or those who have children with a specific diagnosis are urged to 'look beyond the label to see each child' (Macintyre and Deponio, 2003).

It is very important to remember that children display different aspects of a syndrome, for each has a clutch of difficulties which are demonstrated at different levels of severity. The children's difficulties may be mild, moderate or severe and may fluctuate from day to day. This makes accurate diagnosis tricky and explains why children with ostensibly very similar symptoms may be given different 'labels'. Very often the children's difficulties are allowed to obscure their potential so that they do not achieve (in academic or social terms) as well as they might. Frustration and disillusionment for the children and their parents often results. Parents and teachers have to work together to develop strategies to ensure that the positive aspects of each syndrome are developed and the children's self-esteem is not allowed to flounder. School is often an unhappy place for all of these children who have a genuine problem that makes life difficult for them as well as their families and teachers. Looking just the same as other children, those with the difficulties outlined below have a hidden handicap and in the busyness of the school day they are often denied the patience and specialist input they require. Having said that, in many regions an increased awareness has led to many more resource teachers and teaching auxiliaries being employed. They make an invaluable contribution to the children's lives.

ADHD/ADD

- ADHD is a complex neurological condition which results in children having significant problems with concentration, hyperactivity and impulsivity.

- There are two distinctly different kinds. The first has key factors of impulsivity and hyperactivity, the second (often known as ADD) predominantly houses inattention.

- Five per cent of children are thought to have ADHD with a boy : girl ratio 5 : 1. Boys tend to be more aggressive while more girls have the inattentive form and so may be under-diagnosed (Learning Assessment and Neurocare Centre, (www.lanc.uk.com)).

- Two-thirds of children with ADHD will have at least one other coexisting condition such as dyslexia or depression or acute anxiety.

- The children often have developmental delay and need parental/teacher support for longer than their peers.

- Children may have little appreciation of cause and effect so 'future rewards' as bribes to behave have little effect. They are slower to learn skills such as self-management/problem-solving/coping with change.

- Medical assessment may lead to children having medication or nutritional supplements to try to control their restlessness or inattention. This may take time to have an effect.

Dyspraxia

The predominant difficulties within dyspraxia are poor movement planning and organisation that lead to movements being poorly executed. As movement is pervasive and implicit in all learning activities, e.g. speaking and writing, as well as the more obvious physical skills such as catching a ball, tying laces or riding a bike, children with dyspraxia often see themselves as 'stupid' when indeed this is not the case. Their self-esteem suffers because they find it difficult to do the same things as their friends at the same time. They feel vulnerable and confused because they – and indeed many adults – are unsure what is wrong.

Although in education the term dyspraxia is used (to sit alongside dyslexia, dysgraphia and dyscalculia), the term 'developmental co-ordination disorder' is used in the diagnostic and statistical manual (DSM-IV) of the American Psychiatric Association. Five criteria for this are outlined:

■ There is a marked impairment in the development of motor co-ordination.

■ The impairment significantly interferes with academic achievement or activities of daily living.

■ The co-ordination difficulties are not due to a general medical condition, e.g. cerebral palsy, hemiplegia or muscular dystrophy.

■ It is not a pervasive developmental disorder.

■ If developmental delay is evident, the motor difficulties are in excess of those usually associated with it.

As in other specific learning difficulties, boys feature more than girls – in the ratio 4 : 1. Routine and timetables to help planning and organisation that leads to independence are essential. The children must carry out every movement as a first time try and this means they are constantly on the alert and tire very quickly. They have difficulty with hand dominance and crossing the midline of the body. An interesting feature is that often children seem unable to use feedback from one attempt to help the next. They need much appropriate practice at a time when they are fresh. This could be one manifestation of a poor short-term memory that is also part of the condition. Adults should do whatever they can to remove the stress of the day and not burden the children with homework that often means repetition of failure and arguments at home!

Many children lack muscle tone and they have to 'fight' to control their limbs. Constant effort may cause them to withdraw or be resentful, even aggressive. The underlying cause should not be missed.

Dyslexia

Dyslexia is a difficulty with information processing. Many people associate dyslexia with reading and spelling skills, but now it is recognised that many areas of perception and learning are affected. Poor organising and planning skills, a poor concept of time, poor short-term memory, auditory and visual perception (recognising symbols and so affecting reading and mathematics) and spoken language – all of these *may* be present in children with dyslexia. Some children actually see letters move on the page yet may not realise that other readers do not have this visual difficulty.

There is no one definition that covers all children with dyslexia because each child has his or her own blend of difficulties. Many have difficulty in distinguishing different sounds (phonics) and as this affects both spelling and reading it is often when these difficulties become apparent that the possibility of dyslexia is raised. New technology such as MRI scans confirms that there are neurological differences in these children which cause difficulties with language-based activities. It is now claimed that 50 per cent of children with dyslexia have co-occurring dyspraxia.

As more and more children present with these specific learning difficulties, it is essential that ways to support them are found. Adults have to understand and 'live in the skin' of children so that they understand the debilitating features that must be endured. They have also to devise strategies to remove some of the stress of the day. These can be quite straightforward, e.g. giving privacy within the classroom, or extra time to finish work or time out when events of the day threaten to overwhelm. Letting the affected children out to the toilet ahead of the rush, not insisting that they learn unnecessary things, ensuring they have a reliable buddy to show them around – all of these practices can reduce the stress of the day. Above all these children have to have their strengths recognised and enhanced so that they reach their potential in a happy atmosphere of calm endeavour.

Glossary of commonly used terms

ABD. Atypical brain development – a biological basis for learning difficulties.

ADD. Difficulty in holding attention/concentrating; distractibility.

ADHD. As for ADD plus hyperactivity.

Apraxia. Poor motor planning (praxis).

Articulation. The production of language, i.e. vowels and consonants used appropriately and clearly by the active and passive articulators in the mouth (active: soft palate, lips and tongue; passive: hard palate, teeth).

Asperger's syndrome. Difficulty with communication skills.

Auditory sense. Ability to hear clearly, to discriminate sounds which are similar and different, to hold the sounds in the memory long enough to act upon them in some way.

Balance. Static balance: the ability to hold the body steady. Dynamic balance: the ability to be controlled in movement.

Bilateral integration. The ability to co-ordinate two sides of the body (doing different things) to carry out a task, e.g. scoring a goal/basket.

Body awareness/body concept. Knowing through feeling rather than seeing where each body part is in relation to the others and to outside objects (also called body scheme); the internal picture one has of one's own body.

Cluttering. Very quick speech resulting in mumbling.

Co-occurrence. The overlap of symptoms among different conditions.

Co-ordination. The ability to move different body parts efficiently and effectively in different environments.

Critical learning periods. The times when specific skills are learned most readily.

DAMP. Deficit in attention, motor control and perception (Scandinavian term).

Development. The changing patterns (physical, intellectual, emotional, social and motor) which occur sequentially in all children.

Directionality. The ability to appreciate and to move in different directions (forwards, backwards, diagonally and sideways).

Distractibility. Difficulty keeping on task; very short attention span.

Dominance. The preferred side used in tasks such as writing, kicking, opening a jar, etc.

Dysarthria. A condition affecting speech production resulting in slurred speech due to weak or imprecise movement of the speech organs.

Dyscalculia. Poor comprehension of the concept of number and number language.

Dysgraphia. Poor letter formation (due to fine motor disability).

Dyslexia. Difficulty with processing information, particularly reading and spelling.

Dyspraxia. Poor movement planning leading to poor co-ordination.

Fine motor skills. The patterns which depend on the dexterity of the small muscle groups, e.g. picking up and replacing an object, writing, computing, speaking, blinking, etc.

Floppiness. Poor muscle tone allowing too much laxity in the joints making control difficult.

Gross motor skill. Movements which require co-ordination of the large muscle groups, e.g. walking, crawling, jumping.

IEP. Individualised educational plan; required for children who need differentiated work.

Habituation. The ability to recall and reuse items stored in the memory automatically, i.e. without detailed planning.

Kinaesthetic development. Increasing spatial awareness helping efficient movement and directionality.

Maturation. The inbuilt changes that happen in development.

Midline. A strong sense of the midline of the body helps balanced movements as it provides spatial cues (distance and direction). Crossing the midline can be extremely difficult for children with poor hand or foot dominance. Tasks at the midline of the body, e.g. opening a jar, fastening a coat, wiping at the toilet, are problematic for many children with specific learning difficulties.

Motherese. Infant directed speech. Usually slower in pace and higher in pitch.

Myelin. Material forming a sheath around most axons. Not complete at birth.

Myelination. The process by which myelin is added to the axons.

Neurones. The second major class of cells in the nervous system. Responsible for reception and transmission of nerve impulses.

Perception. The brain's ability to make sense of information coming from the environment through the different senses.

Phonological awareness. Ability to hear the separate sounds within words.

Posture. The alignment of body parts during movement and in stillness.

Praxis. The ability to move efficiently and effectively in different environments.

Proprioception. The sensory input from nerve endings in the muscles which pass information about movement – where and how it is occurring.

Reflex. Involuntary movement in response to a stimulus and the concurrent physiological process.

Reflex inhibition programme. Individual programmes to inhibit primitive reflexes which are hindering the development of postural ones.

Self-concept. The image one has of one's self – physical, social, emotional and intellectual.

Self-esteem. A global judgement of self-worth gained by comparing self to the personal notion of the ideal.

Sensory integration. The ability to select and co-ordinate the information (input) coming from the environment (through the receptors in the body to the brain) to produce efficient and effective output.

Sequencing. The ability to order steps and stages so that they flow together in the correct order.

Skilled movement. The correct selection of strength, speed and space to provide momentum with control resulting in effective output.

SLI. Specific language impairment – concerns all children with an abnormality in their grasp of spoken language.

SNAP. A new computer aided diagnostic assessment tool for special needs. www.hoddertests.co.uk

Spatial orientation. The ability to judge distances and directions so that positioning the body in relation to outside objects is secure.

Tactile defensiveness. An extreme reaction to being touched or having personal space 'invaded'.

Tone. Appropriate muscle strength for the task to be done: hyper = too much; hypo = too little.

Tracking. Also called smooth pursuit. The ability of the eyes to follow pathways smoothly.

Vestibular sense. The sense that feeds positional information to the brain. Essential for balanced movement/stillness.

Visual sense. Used to recognise people, objects, distances and depths; objects as distinct from their background; parts from a whole object; relationships between people and objects; stimulates hand–eye co-ordination; helps learning by providing visual memory.

Bibliography

Ainsworth, M. (1972) 'Attachment and dependency: a comparison', in J. and L. Gerewitz (eds), *Attachment and Dependency*. Washington, DC: V.H. Winston.

Alston, J. (1996) 'Assessing and promoting handwriting skills', in G. Reid (ed.), *Dimensions of Dyslexia*, Vol. 2. Edinburgh: Moray House.

Ashcroft, J.R. and Chinn S.J. (1992) *Dyslexia and Mathematics*. London: Routledge.

Ausubel, D.P. (1963) *School Learning: An Introduction to Educational Psychology*. London: Holt Reinhart & Winston.

Ayres, J. (1972) *Sensory Integration and Learning Disorders*. Los Angeles: Western Psychological Services.

Bee, H. (1999) *Lifespan Development*. Harlow: Longman.

Bee, H. (2001) *The Growing Child*. New York: Addison Wesley Educational.

Bowlby, J. (1979) *The Making and Breaking of Affectational Bonds*. London: Tavistock Press.

Brown, P. and Chamove, J.O. (1993) 'Working in harmony with how people change naturally', *The Weight Control Digest*, 3 (3).

Bruner, J.S. (1966) *The Process of Education*. Cambridge, MA: Harvard University Press.

Buzan, T. (1993) *The Mind Map Book*. London: BBC Worldwide.

Cohen, D. (1996) *The Importance of Play*. New York: University Press.

Cooley, C. (1962) *Human Nature and the Social Order*. New York: Charles Scribner.

Cowden, J.E. and Euston, B.L. (1991) 'Pediatric adapted physical education for infants, toddlers and pre-school children', *Adapted Physical Education Quarterly*, 8: 263–79.

Craig, G. (2002) *Information on ADHD*. Edinburgh: North West Edinburgh ADHD Pilot Project.

de Buitleir, F. (2003) 'But dyslexia only affects words, doesn't it? – A consideration of maths and the dyslexic learner', in *LearnJournal*, journal of the Irish Learning Support Association, Vol. 25.

Dehaene, S. and Spelke, E. (2003) Science Section, *Daily Telegraph*, 3 September.

Department for Education and Employment (2000) *Curriculum Guidance for the Foundation Stage*. London: DfEE.

Dobie, S. (1996) 'Perceptual-motor and neurodevelopmental dimensions', in G. Reid (ed.), *Dimensions of Dyslexia*, Vol. 2. Edinburgh: Moray House.

Flavell, J.H., Miller, P.H. and Miller, S.A. (1992) *Cognitive Development*, 3rd edn. Englewood Cliffs, NJ: Prentice Hall.

Gallahue, D. (1993) *Developmental Physical Education for Today's Children*. Dubuque, IA: Brown Communications.

Goddard, S. (1996) *A Teacher's Window into the Child's Mind*. Eugene, OR: Fern Ridge Press.

Goddard, S. (2002) *Reflexes, Learning and Behavior: A Window into the Child's Mind*. Eugene, OR: Fern Ridge Press.

Green, D., Henderson, S., Barnett, A. and Baird, G. (2000) 'The clumsiness in children with developmental co-ordination disorder and Asperger's syndrome – same or different?', in *Stepping Forward*, conference proceedings of the Dyspraxia Foundation.

HMI (1997) *A Curriculum Framework for Children in Their Pre-school Year*. Edinburgh: Scottish Office.

Hornsby, B. (1984) *Discovering Dyslexia*. London: Martin Dunitz.

Kaplan, B., Dewey, D.M., Crawford, S.G. and Wilson, B.N. (2001) 'The term co-morbidity is of questionable value in reference to developmental disorders: data and theory', *Journal of Learning Disabilities*, 34 (6).

Keen, D. (2001) *Specific Neurodevelopmental Disorders*. Paper presented at the conference on the needs of children with specific developmental difficulties, Bishop Aukland.

Kiely, M. (1996) 'Handwriting – skills strategies and success' in G. Reid (ed.), *Dimensions of Dyslexia*, Vol. 2. Edinburgh: Moray House.

Kirby, A. and Drew, S. (2002) *Guide to Dyspraxia and Developmental Co-ordination Disorders*. London: David Fulton.

Laban, R. (1942) The Mastery of Movement, 4th edn. London: Macdonald & Evans.

Laszlo, J.I. and Bairstow, P.J. (1985) *Perceptual-Motor Behaviour, Assessment and Therapy*. London: Holt, Reinhart & Winston.

Levine, M. (1994) *Educational Care*. Cambridge, MA: Educators Publishing Service.

Macintyre, C. (2000) *Enhancing Learning through Play*. London: David Fulton.

Macintyre, C. (2001) *The Art of Action Research in the Classroom*. London: David Fulton.

Macintyre, C. and Deponio, P. (2003) *Assessing and Supporting Children with Specific Learning Difficulties. Looking beyond the Label to Assess the Whole Child*. London: Routledge.

Macintyre, C. and McVitty, K. (2003) *Planning the Pre-5 Setting*. London: David Fulton.

Macintyre, C. and Murdoch, E. (1985) *Assessment in Physical Education*, SEED funded research report, Dunfermline College, Edinburgh.

National Deaf Children's Society (2003) *Stop Bullying*. Available at http://www.ndcs.org.uk.

Olweus, D. (1995) 'Bullying or peer abuse at school: facts and intervention', *Current Directions in Psychological Science*, 4.

Payne, S. (1998) 'Occupational therapy: the dyspraxic child at secondary school', in *Praxis Makes Perfect II*. Hitchin: Dyspraxia Foundation.

Piaget, J. (1977) *The Development of Thought: Equilibration of Cognitive Structures*. New York: Viking Press.

Pyfer, J. and Johnson, R. (1981) 'Factors affecting motor delays', *Adapted Physical Education*. Eason, Smith and Carron, Human Kinetics publishers Box 5076 Champaign, 111 61820.

Sassoon, R. (1998) 'Dealing with handwriting problems', in *Praxis Makes Perfect II*. Hitchin: Dyspraxia Foundation.

Scottish Consultative Council on the Curriculum (1999) *A Curriculum Framework for Children 3–5*. Edinburgh: SCCC.

Scottish Executive (2000) *The Child at the Centre*. Edinburgh: Scottish Office.

Sharma, M. (1990) *Dyslexia, Dyscalculia and Some Remedial Perspectives for Mathematical Problems*. Framingham, MA: Center for Teaching and Learning Mathematics.

Stein, J. (2000) 'The magnocellular theory of developmental dyslexia', *Dyslexia*, 7: 12–36.

Stordy, B.J. (1997) 'Dyslexia, attention hyperactivity disorder – do fatty acids help?', *Dyslexia Review*, 9 (2).

Thomas, A. and Chess, S. (1977) *Temperament and Development*. New York: Bruner Mazel.

Trevarthen, C. (1977) *Play for Tomorrow*. Edinburgh: Video Production Unit, University of Edinburgh.

Vygotsky, L.S. (1978) *Mind and Society*. Cambridge, MA: Oxford University Press.

Wheedon, C. and Reid, G. (2003) SNAP– Computer aided diagnostic assessment. www.hoddertests.co.uk.

Winkley, D. (2003) *Grey Matters: Current Neurological Research and Its Implications for Educators*. Available at http//www.keele.ac.uk/depts/ed/kisnet/interviews/winkley.htm.

Winston, Professor R. (2003) *The Human Mind*. BBC1.

Index